D0119397

# The Making of the Central Pennines

## John Porter

MOORLAND PUBLISHING CO.

British Library Cataloguing in Publication Data

Porter, John
    The making of the Central Pennines.
    1. Pennine Chain
    I. Title
    942.8          DA670.P4

    ISBN 0-903485-80-X

ISBN 0 903485 80 X

Typeset by Alacrity Phototypesetters,
Banwell Castle, Weston-super-Mare, Avon
and printed in Great Britain by
Redwood Burn Ltd, Trowbridge and Esher for
Moorland Publishing Co Ltd,
9-11 Station Street, Ashbourne, Derbyshire

# Contents

# Illustrations

# Preface

An early life spent in east Lancashire, followed by several years of living away from this area, has convinced me that the landscape of the central Pennines is among the most distinctive in Britain. One reason for its unique character is the close association between town and country, for few urban areas in the region are not within a short drive of open countryside and some are directly overlooked by fine, open moorlands. The most enjoyable aspect of writing this book has been the opportunity it has provided to see so much of the region out of doors at first hand — yet no matter how much is seen, there always remains so much more to see. The inspiration of the book, throughout its preparation, has been the landscape.

The bibliography of the central Pennine landscape is prolific, much of the literature being contained within the transactions of county historical societies and in works now often out of print. For these reasons I have included not a full bibliography but a selection of items for further reading. Some are general introductions to the subject, while others enable the reader to follow up a specific aspect in more detail. Much can be learned about the history of particular places from the growing volume of leaflets and guides issued by local museums, libraries, and civic societies; the town trails available for Barrowford, Haworth, and Heptonstall are examples of especially informative items. Moreover local historical groups now frequently issue bulletins or newsletters which contain a wealth of detail about the history of particular buildings and other landscape features.

The materials and information required for this book have come from many sources. I should like to thank the West Yorkshire County Council for supplying information on recreational planning; and J.M. Till for allowing me to use his material on Newtown, including Figure 24. Further acknowledgements are due to Blackburn Libraries and Museums (Figs 11 and 18), the Borough of Bolton Arts Department (Fig 15), the Lancashire County Museum Service (Fig 46), the Lancashire Record Office (Fig 12), and the Public Record Office (Fig 40, from document DL44 468). Figure 39 is from the muniments of the Parker family deposited in the Lancashire Record Office (ref DDB 84/1), and Figure 9 is from the Slaidburn manorial records deposited in the same office by the Lord of the Manor, the Hon Nicholas Assheton.

Finally, this has been a book in which family, friends, and colleagues have been very forthcoming with practical help. I am particularly grateful to Ron Riley for his time and patience in the production of the ink sketches. The photographs have benefited from Michael Flanagan's careful processing, and the text is the better for the critical comments of my wife, Margaret, on my use and misuse of the English language. Final thanks are due to Aileen Gerstel and Pat Lay, who between them performed the onerous task of typing most of the manuscript. Any errors or misinterpretations are of course my own responsibility.

JOHN PORTER
Farnborough,
Hampshire.

# 1 Introduction: A Pennine Panorama

The most prominent relief feature of northern England, stretching from the Scottish border to the valley of the Trent, is the long range of hills and moorlands known as the Pennines. North of the Trent and excluding the Lake District there are few places west of the Lincolnshire and Yorkshire Wolds from which a Pennine skyline is not visible on a clear day. The aspect of this chain of hills is varied: high rounded summits alternate with lower moorland plateaux, and variations in rock type and structure divide the chain into principal ranges, each with its distinctive scenery. Although much of this scenery is still natural, over the centuries the hand of man has taken an increasing role in shaping the landscape. This is particularly true along the Pennine edges, which are among the most densely populated parts of Britain.

Astride the old boundary between Lancashire and Yorkshire lies a portion of the Pennines where the hand of man has been especially active in fashioning the landscape. This is the central Pennines, an area stretching from Bradford and Huddersfield in the east to Lancaster and Chorley in the west (Fig 1). The southern boundary is at Standedge on the marches of the Peak District; the northern boundary is the valley of the Aire, separating the region from Wharfedale and the Yorkshire Dales National Park beyond. The region is not wholly upland but is broken by the broad valleys of the Ribble and Lancashire Calder. On both the eastern and western side streams have cut deep valleys into the moorland edges and here towns and industries have taken root. The central Pennines are thus flanked by some of the most extensive urban areas of Britain; large portions lie within the metropolitan counties of West Yorkshire and Greater Manchester while most of the remainder overlooks the large industrial towns of north Lancashire. It is not surprising therefore that man should have made deep and not always pleasant marks on the landscape; yet despite the scars the region still presents a handsome face to those who pause to scrutinise it.

One region of the central Pennines still preserving most of its natural character lies between Littleborough and Ripponden. From Littleborough an old paved road, thought by some to date back to the Roman age and by others to belong to the later packhorse era, winds its way up on to the high ridge between Lancashire and Yorkshire at Blackstone Edge. Daniel Defoe toiled up this slope about 1720 and wrote about its awesome mountainous nature in his *Tour Through the Whole Island of Great Britain*. The ridge he crossed is the crest of the main central Pennine axis, a dissected belt of high plateaux and rounded summits stretching from Standedge in the south to Lothersdale in the north. The coarse sandstones of the Millstone Grit Series comprising this range of moors were once covered by Coal Measures, but about three hundred million years ago the range was thrust upwards and then planed down by the weather and stream action. The overlying Coal Measures were completely worn away except along the eastern and western flanks leaving the hard gritstones to form the high central ridge. Along the edge the gritstones outcrop as a skyline of angular boulders and crags which overlook steep slopes covered with rough moorland grass stretching down into the head of the Roch valley. At the summit is the remains of the Aiggin Stone, a stone cross of great antiquity which gave direction and comfort to travellers in earlier times. Resting upon one of the boulders of the edge by the cross stone, the present-day traveller sits upon the roof of England

1    The Central Pennines: major towns and principal physical features.

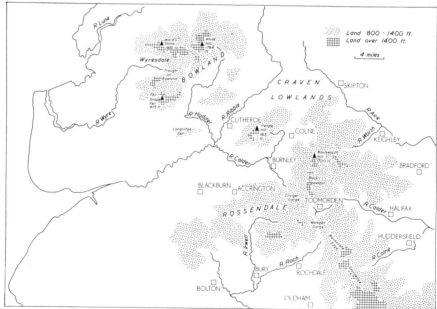

2 Pennine landscape: high moorland at Cliviger.

and soon finds detachment from the hectic bustle of urban life below.

The solitude however is often deceptive. The walker is soon likely to be joined by others, for along the edge there now runs a route especially designed to further the enjoyment of the Pennine moors by the townsman. This is the Pennine Way, a national long-distance footpath which every year attracts an increasing number of people to the central Pennines. Turning north along this path the walker soon reaches the busy A58 Rochdale to Halifax road, which path then passes the Blackstone Edge Reservoir, one of six built originally to keep the Rochdale canal supplied with water at the summit pass below, but now used to provide water for Rochdale. The central Pennines have seen a proliferation of reservoirs to satisfy the needs of the growing conurbations below, for the level surfaces of impervious gritstones are ideal for water retention and there are few areas along the main Pennine axis which are not now used as reservoir catchments. The walker passes further reservoirs before the Pennine Way swings eastwards to the 120ft-high Stoodley Pike monument built to commemorate the abdication of Napoleon in 1814. The monument stands on a ridge 1,300ft above sea level and has a commanding view across the Calder valley.

The Calder valley between Todmorden and Halifax shows in an often quite dramatic form many aspects of the interaction between man and the Pennine environment. The valley itself is narrow and steep sided, and alongside the river a main road, canal, and railway cross and re-cross as they struggle to find space. Beside these arteries, first built to carry the traffic of the Industrial Revolution, straggle remains of the Victorian industrial scene — empty mills, narrow streets, rows of terraced houses, and nonconformist chapels. At Todmorden and Hebden Bridge old public buildings stand as a monument to an age of prosperity long past, their once dignified stone frontages blackened by a century of exposure to the soot-laden atmosphere. The valley could not contain all the urban expansion within its confines, and so the houses and mills spread into the mouths of tributary valleys and up on to the hillsides. Yet along its length the scene is never wholly urban; those steep valley sides which are heavily wooded have a pastoral aspect. Where the valley widens the rural vista is reinforced by the lines of stone walling upon the spreading moors beyond.

The deeply incised nature of the Calder means that its tributaries join it down very steep gradients. The lanes leading up these valleys often find no space along the precipitous slopes and follow circuitous routes to reach the small, scattered communities higher up. They link together settlements which were in existence many centuries before those of the main valley below. Luddenden has its mills and Victorian terraces, but the mills are pre-Victorian water mills and the village itself was a thriving hand-weaving community long before the Industrial Revolution. Above Luddenden the moors are criss-crossed by a network of old roads which serve handsome stone farmhouses and cottages with long ranges of mullioned windows and finely carved datestones, built for the most part in the seventeenth and eighteenth centuries and standing in small fields divided by dry stone walls. They show that the district was well populated by a society of farmers and hand weavers many years before the growth of industries and towns along the Calder and the old packhorse tracks along the hillsides were the routes by which the wool and cloth were collected from, and distributed to, the many scattered homesteads. Some valleys are now deserted with their old mill sites overgrown and almost wholly disappeared; Hardcastle Crags along the Hebden Water above Hebden Bridge is a now wholly wooded valley with a rich profusion of plant life covering vanished mill sites and with a maze of woodland paths and trails along its length.

North of the Calder towards Denholme and Keighley lie the moors drained by the Worth valley. This is the country revealed to a wider world through the novels of the Brontë sisters. Haworth itself is a fine ridge top village recorded in medieval times and its building fabric dates from the seventeenth and eighteenth centuries: it would be worthy of note even without the Brontës. A walk on the nearby moors and around neighbouring villages soon reveals aspects of the personality of the region which have made it world famous through the writings of the sisters — especially the rapid and frequent changes of the landscape from tranquillity to wilderness and the impact of this temperamental environment on its isolated and inward-looking inhabitants. Not far from Haworth almost upon the main Pennine watershed are the old farmhouses which can be identified with the dwellings in Emily Brontë's novel, *Wuthering Heights*. These moors can be hazardous to walkers once thick cloud has settled over the summits, and bog bursts sometimes occur after heavy rain, the most well known being that of 1824 when the saturated peat-covered surface of Crow Hill could contain no more rainwater and the bog burst out of the moor with a roar heard for miles around. The village of Ponden was covered to a depth of several feet, and so impressed with the occurrence was the Reverend Patrick Brontë that he preached a sermon based on the text, 'The hills melted like wax at the presence of the Lord, at the presence of the Lord the whole earth'. East of

3   Pennine landscape: the river Hodder at Newton. Moorlands often intersperse with picturesque valleys.

a line drawn between Halifax and Keighley the gritstone plateaux pass into the lower moors of the Lower Coal Measures Series. The soil has the same sterile quality but supports walled pastures; farms fill in the spaces between old mill or mining villages, and the receding Pennine edge becomes submerged beneath the growing suburbs of Bradford.

West of the main Pennine fold lies a range of moors formed from the same rocks but with a more complex geological structure. Here up-thrusting similar to that which occurred further east, but instead along an east to west axis, produced the moorlands of the Forest of Rossendale. The landscape is similar to the Calder valley region with deep valleys cutting through the gritstones and Coal Measures, and each valley is occupied by a straggling column of textile mills and terraced houses. The alternation of hard gritstones and softer shales in the structure gives parts of the landscape a stepped appearance, the weak shales being worn back into the hillsides while the gritstones stand out as benches. Dry stone walls largely dating from the seventeenth century carve the landscape into small fields, each group of two or three such fields being occupied by a cottage or small farmhouse originating from the same period. As along the Calder valley, old lanes high on the valley sides link hill hamlets and villages. Industrial towns such as Blackburn, Burnley, and Bolton spread up on to the edges of Rossendale transforming some of its old hamlets into modern commuter settlements. There are still, however, many expanses of fine, unspoilt moorland along these western Pennine fringes; from the summit of the Victoria Jubilee Tower on Darwen Moor the view to the south and west takes in the open, unfenced moorlands, the freedom of which was won by the people of Darwen at the end of the last century. Beyond the moors lies the Lancashire plain, and on a very clear day the Fylde coast is visible.

North of the Rossendale upland lies the valley of the Ribble and its tributary, the Lancashire Calder. The Ribble valley cuts a broad swathe through the western Pennines, relieving the windswept moorland scenery by a belt of fertile hedged pastures and wooded vales occupied by attractive villages such as Hurst Green and Downham. Above the clay floored plain rise low hillocks or knolls of limestone, and from its site on one of these the Norman-built Clitheroe castle commands a view across the market town at its feet towards the moors of Bowland and Pendle rising sharply from the valley floor. The most striking feature of the view from Clitheroe castle is the stark profile of Pendle Hill, its grim gritstone-capped edge conveying the sense of mystery and foreboding which once contributed towards its association with witchcraft. On the other side of Pendle the ground falls away less steeply but the relief remains hilly; moorland eventually gives way to farmland, and the lower slopes of Pendle are a tangle of old winding lanes joining scattered hamlets and small industrial villages along the edge of Burnley and its neighbouring towns.

Just south of Clitheroe the Ribble is joined by another tributary, the Hodder. This river leads northwards into an outlying portion of the Pennines known as Bowland, a massif of Millstone Grit rising to summits in excess of 1,500 ft, the highest in the central Pennines. The Hodder drains the south-eastern side of Bowland and passes through some of the most remote and unspoilt scenery in northern England. Here, in contrast to the Pennine regions further south, industrial growth barely reached the cottage industry stage and it is possible to find evidence of twelve or more centuries of continuous rural life. The lower parts of Bowland around Whitewell and Chipping comprise a tangle of hedges, low walls, and winding country lanes joining many scattered small farms. The scenery has a park-like quality echoing a period long past when it was royal forest. Villages are few but ancient, and their parishes large. Towards the centre of the upland the scenery takes on a mountainous

4   Pennine landscape: the urban scene at Hebden Bridge. Mills and terraced houses crowd the valley floor and steep hillsides. The terraces have one house above the other.

aspect, the gritstone being dissected by the swift-flowing streams of the upper Hodder and its tributaries. In these remote valleys there are several farms lying more than three miles from the nearest public road.

The main divide of Bowland is penetrated by a picturesque, steeply winding pass, the Trough of Bowland, and this leads on to the most westerly moors of the central Pennines, a region drained by the headwaters of the Wyre. Here there is a history of continuous settlement and farming since the time of the Norsemen, and the homes of these early pioneers can be found tucked away under the shelter of the fell sides. Wyresdale escaped the blight of the Industrial Revolution although it contains the occasional small mill village along its edge; Calder Vale, with its Victorian terraces, mill, and adjacent chapel, is oddly out of place in this countryside of winding lanes and remote farms, and it is almost as though the Industrial Revolution had arrived there by mistake, and discovering the error quickly departed. The neighbouring fells look across the Fylde plain to the Lancashire coast, and at Lancaster there is a meeting of hill, plain, and sea.

Throughout the central Pennines two elements have contributed to the landscape. The older is the hand of nature, present throughout the region's history and still dominant in the higher, more remote areas. The younger is the hand of man, active for only the most recent fraction of the region's life but having wrought enormous changes, particularly in the more accessible districts where the natural landscape is almost wholly submerged by human artefacts. Even those parts of the Pennines furthest from human settlements are now utilised for man's purposes — they supply the water and breathing spaces for the adjacent sprawling conurbations.

Scrutiny of the Pennine landscape reveals that the interaction between the region and its inhabitants has often been close. Farmhouses and cottages made of local gritstone blend into the scenery and their rugged proportions reflect the bleak environment. Along the hillsides old lanes wind close to the contours searching out the easiest routes, and at their feet the wooded cloughs of streams tumbling off the Pennine edges conceal tiny mill communities once dependent upon the water power for their livelihoods. To trace the origins of this integration between man and the Pennine landscape it is necessary to return to the earliest periods of human settlement.

**Selected further reading:**

H. C. Collins, *South Pennine Park*, Dalesman, 1974

R. Millward, *Lancashire: The History of the Landscape*, Hodder & Stoughton, 1955

A. Raistrick, *The Making of the English Landscape: West Riding of Yorkshire*, Hodder & Stoughton, 1970

# 2 The Coming of Man to the Pennines

High on a spur of the eastern Pennines at Almondbury, six hundred feet above the town of Huddersfield, is a large earthwork. Oval in shape, it consists of a series of ramparts covering about eight acres. By comparison with the scale of landscape alteration undertaken in building the M62 across the Scammonden valley eight miles away, the Almondbury earthwork might be thought of as a modest contribution by man to the Pennine scene. Yet it is the most prominent remain of early man in the Yorkshire Pennines. By prehistoric standards it represents a considerable feat of civil engineering.

One of the reasons why prehistoric remains on the scale of Almondbury are so hard to find in the Pennines is that the region was only sparsely populated by early man, which is not surprising in view of its natural characteristics. In both Lancashire and Yorkshire the lowland vales flanking the Pennines and the deep valleys which scar the craggy edges of the moorlands are covered in thick clay which in prehistoric times supported dense oak forest. Early man had the tools neither to fell these large trees nor to till the heavy soils which lay beneath them. Above the limits of the forest stretched steep moorland edges which levelled out to give windswept, rain-soaked plateaux made impassable by peat bogs. Bronze Age settlers moved under the shadows of the lowland forests and left a trail of bronze implements along their trading routes through Airedale and Ribblesdale. They buried their dead in barrows on the hillsides, but otherwise did little to change the natural landscape.

By about 300 BC a people using iron instead of bronze for their implements had appeared in the Pennine region. These Iron Age settlers, the Celts or Britons, were more numerous than their Bronze Age predecessors and soon established a strong, unified, tribal organisation based on regional capitals to which lesser settlements rendered services and tribute. Although few of their settlements can now be traced their presence is reflected in the many topographical names of British origin, such as the rivers Hodder, Wyre, and Lune, and old regional names such as Craven and Elmet.

The Almondbury earthwork reflects the endeavours of successive prehistoric peoples. The site was first occupied as a defensive camp in Neolithic times. Around the seventh century BC Iron Age man erected the present structure, a hill fort which was widely used in the first Christian century to oppose the Roman invasion. It occupies a commanding position  at the entrance to the Colne valley, and within its ramparts men, women, children and livestock could find refuge from the invaders. The site proved to be so useful for defence that a castle was built inside the earthwork during the reign of Stephen. Celtic hill forts are not common in the central Pennines but another is situated a few miles north on the moors near Haworth. This one has a less spectacular position and is smaller, enclosing about two acres. The semicircular

5   Roman and prehistoric remains. The central Pennines was a frontier region in Roman times. Roads were military supply routes joining forts.

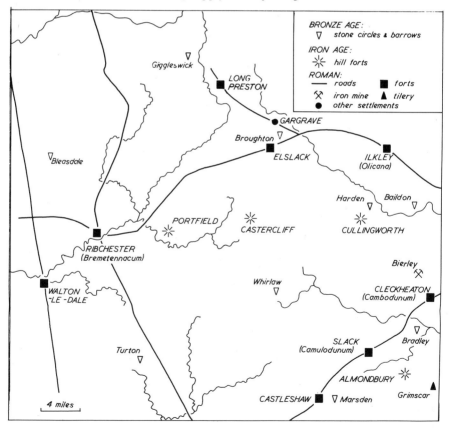

remains of the earthen rampart 6ft high and the ditch 4ft deep are still visible.

The Britons' hill forts, however, proved to be no defence against the Roman legions, which had reduced the Brigantian region to Roman rule by AD85. The subjugation of the Britons did little, however, to alter their way of life. The Roman conquest of northern England was undertaken with the military purpose of securing the more populous lands of the south-east against the unconquered tribes of the north and Scotland. The Romans regarded the lands straddling the Pennines as a frontier zone and made little attempt to settle and 'Romanise' the region. Instead their occupation was largely limited to the construction of forts at key strategic points linked by paved roads along which men and materials could be moved quickly in the event of a military emergency. One of these forts was at Slack on the opposite side of the Colne valley from Almondbury. Here excavation revealed the remains of a rampart enclosing an area of four acres which had contained granaries, barracks, workshops, and a paved parade ground. Slack was one of several forts guarding the road from Manchester to Tadcaster. The greater part of this road, like the majority of Roman Roads, gradually fell into disuse after the Romans left Britain.

Roman roads nevertheless provided the means by which the first Anglian settlers could penetrate the countryside. These Angles began to arrive towards the end of the sixth century almost two hundred years after the end of Roman rule. By the early seventh century groups of Angles were colonising the Pennine valleys of west Yorkshire and moving through Airedale and Ribblesdale into Lancashire. Other Anglian settlers reached south Lancashire from the midland kingdom of Mercia. The settlements of these peoples can be recognised from the occurrence of Old English elements in their place-names. The most characteristic of these elements are -ing, -ham, -tun, -wic, and -word (-worth). All mean a homestead or farm, single settlements which quickly developed into a cluster or nucleus of homesteads. These village names occur in all the valley and lowland regions flanking the Pennines but are especially common in Airedale, Ribblesdale, and lower Calderdale. The Craven lowlands have examples in Long Preston, Wigglesworth, Giggleswick, Horton, and Barnoldswick. Along the Lune and Wenning we find Melling, Austwick, Clapham, Wennington, and Halton.

Although the widespread nature of Old English place-name elements suggests that settlement by these peoples must have been very intensive, caution is required in attributing all villages with these elements to Anglo-Saxon origins. There is evidence to suggest that at the time of the English occupation a strong native British society still existed. Some of the traditional land tenure customs of the region practised in medieval times have a striking affinity with those of medieval Wales and other areas of Celtic culture. This suggests that Celtic society, far from being submerged by the English invasion, survived the occupation in sufficient strength to contribute to the social framework of later centuries. It is unlikely that the settlements of such a society would have disappeared at the time of the English colonisation to make way for the new villages of the invaders. Instead the English may well have imposed their own occupation on an already existing settlement pattern, taking over British villages and re-naming them in their own language.

The siting of early villages reflected many considerations. Dry foundations within a few yards of a regular supply of fresh water were needed. Villagers also required to be within walking distance of land providing tillage, meadowland, woodland and rough pasture. We can envisage each village in its early years as a cluster of perhaps no more than half a dozen homesteads, each house comprising a long single room shared by man and animals alike. The village sites of today may not be exactly the same as those originally chosen since the first settlers would have been unlikely to find the best sites immediately. The early years of settlement would have been marked by frequent changes of house site, perhaps only a few yards at a time, until as a result of long experience of local conditions a particular location was found to be the most satisfactory and became permanent.

By Anglian times the transformation of the woodland landscape of the Pennine valleys was well under way. Gradually the native forests were cleared and replaced by a pattern of tilled fields and pastures divided up by a network of hedges. The first clearances took place immediately around the villages themselves. As their populations grew, the tilled area was expanded, but for centuries to come each village was separated from its neighbours by tracts of uncleared forest. Already some of the settlements which were to achieve great industrial importance in later years had appeared; the names of Bolton, Blackburn and Bradford were as familiar to the early English as they are today.

The descendants of the English settlers were well established when, in the early tenth century, they were joined by new colonisers from Denmark and Norway. The Danish colonisation came from the east, and its main impact was in lowland Yorkshire, where the Danes added to the already existing pattern of villages. Earby, Skipton, and Sowerby are examples of their settlements. The Norsemen, however, who reached the Lancashire coast from existing colonies in Ireland and the Isle of Man, added a more distinctive element to the landscape. They came from an environment of small, isolated farms, mountainous terrain, and poor land, and their Pennine settlements reflect this background. They penetrated the upper valleys of the western Pennines, founding farms and hamlets and grazing their cattle and sheep on the rough moorland pastures.

As with the English settlement, place-name evidence reveals something of the pattern of the Norse occupation. In Bowland outside Slaidburn is a large house called Dunnow. The house occupies the site of a former settlement called Battersby which is recorded as early as the Domesday Book, and in the sixteenth century had no fewer than eight farmers. The name is of Norse origin and means the *byr* or homestead of one Bathar, a Norse chief. Just over two miles away, the farm of Beatrix nestles under the shelter of the high Bowland fells. Beatrix is derived from *Batherarghes*, another Norse name meaning the shieling or hill farm of Bathar. It seems that in the tenth century these farms belonged to the same Norseman, cattle from Battersby being regularly pastured around Beatrix. Sometimes Norse farmers regularly drove livestock from the main homestead on to higher pastures for summer grazing to be watched over by a shepherd or cowman who remained for periods with the herds. This occurred in Wyresdale on the far side of the Bowland fells, where there is a farm called Ortner, formerly *Overtonergh*, the *ergh* or shieling of the settlement of Overton on the sands of the Lune estuary. The survival of this name suggests that in this remote period, almost wholly unrecorded by the written word, Viking farmers who had settled at the mouth of the Lune regularly drove their cattle across the sands of the estuary at low tide to summer grazings in the hills of Wyresdale six miles away. The frequent occurrence in this region of Norse terms such as *-gil* (ravine) and *-slack* (hollow) which passed into later English usage testifies to the impact of the Norse settlement.

In the eleventh century a new power came to the Pennines. The Norman lords stamped their authority upon the barren fells and wooded valleys, endeavouring to mould the diverse peoples and equally varied traditions and institutions to a new feudal order. The symbols of their power were the castles of Lancaster, Skipton, Clitheroe and Wakefield, strategically located to survey the wide, surrounding moorland expanses and the activities and movements of the inhabitants. Each castle was the administrative centre of an extensive feudal estate; the manor of Wakefield for example comprised forty-seven villages as well as smaller hamlets and dispersed farms, and many of these settlements lay far from the castle in the upper Calder and Colne valleys. Under the protection of these castles early market towns developed. Clitheroe in the Ribble valley grew up around the Norman castle which stands on a limestone knoll rising some fifty feet above the valley floor (Fig 6). The castle was built by Ilbert de Lacy, lord of the Honour of Clitheroe, in about 1100. From the top of its square keep, the only part now surviving,

6 Clitheroe Castle. The Norman castle of the Lacy family overlooks this old market town of the Ribble valley and the moorland fells beyond.

the Lacy lords of the Honour could survey the trading activities of the town and look beyond to their tributary villages and hamlets along the Ribble valley and in the hills of Bowland and Pendle.

By Norman times a further new feature was beginning to appear in the landscape. Until the eleventh and twelfth centuries Christian churches had been few and far between. The pre-Norman churches at Lancaster and Whalley ministered to vast parishes in which the majority of people lived at great distances from the church itself and so gathered for worship at wayside stone preaching crosses. The pre-Conquest parish of Whalley stretched almost thirty miles across east Lancashire from the heights of Bowland to the plateaux of the main Pennine watershed at Cliviger. At the time of the compilation of the Domesday Book in 1086 no fewer than fifty vills or townships lay within its boundaries. The Normans, however, were great benefactors of the Church, using their ecclesiastical patronage to strengthen their secular power. In the decades following the Conquest they founded several new churches and chapels in the Pennines, and new parish churches at Blackburn, Mitton and Slaidburn were carved out of the parish of Whalley. By 1300 the ancient mother church itself, with the aid of its Norman patrons, had founded dependent chapelries at Downham, Colne, Burnley, Altham, Clitheroe and Haslingden. Yet even with these foundations, several lowland villages still lay three or more miles from a place of worship, while the farmsteads of the remote uplands lay at even greater distances.

7   The Honour of Clitheroe, a medieval Pennine estate. The Honour, administered from the castle at Clitheroe and a manor house at Ightenhill, comprised some sixty villages besides many hamlets and isolated farms. Several villages formed part of the lord's demesne. The five forests were originally hunting grounds but were later used for cattle rearing, the deer being restricted to enclosed parks.

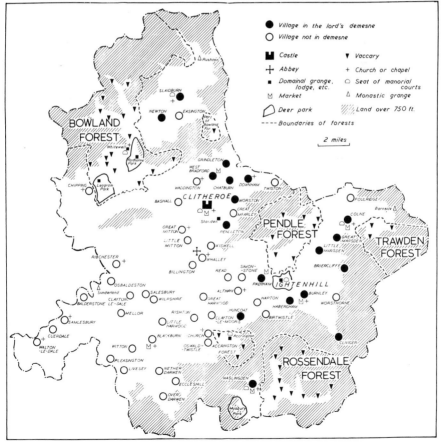

Houses of the great religious orders appeared in the lower Pennine valleys. The Cistercians founded abbeys at Kirkstall, Kirklees, Esholt, Sawley, Whalley and Wyresdale. Kirkstall, now a district of Leeds, was founded by a colony of monks from Fountains. They first settled at Barnoldswick, but after disagreements with their secular neighbours moved to the Airedale site. Whalley Abbey was founded in 1294 by monks from Stanlow in Cheshire. Sawley was established by twelve monks and ten lay brethren from Fountains but the house did not prosper because of the cold, damp weather which the monks claimed rotted their crops on the stalk. Abandonment of the site was prevented only by gifts of land and churches from Matilda de Percy, countess of Warwick, daughter of the founder. She found the Ribble valley to be 'foggy and rainy country' with an 'ungenial air, hunger, and a want of all necessities through general poverty.'

The abbeys were not merely communities of brothers but were also great landed enterprises, for land was essential to bring in an income and make the house self-sufficient in foodstuffs. Some lands were let to laymen but others were worked by the monks themselves and their lay brethren as demesne farms or granges, of which there were several in the Pennines, particularly in Yorkshire. Most of Kirkstall's granges lay within eight miles north and east of the abbey, and although now suburbs of Leeds, in some cases the site of the Abbey's farms can still be traced from the occurrence of 'grange' names on the modern map — as in the case of Roundhay Grange, Breary Grange and Rigton Grange. Kirkstall also had granges much further away at Cliviger, Accrington, Barnoldswick and Rushton in Bowland.

The Rushton lands of Kirkstall lay nearly forty miles from the mother house. Rushton, which now lies submerged beneath the Stocks-in-Bowland reservoir, was granted to the Kirkstall monks in 1180 by Robert de Lacy, who also provided them with pasture for 160 mares and their two-yearlings and for 200 cows with their three-year-old offspring. His successors followed this up with other grants of land in 1220 and 1235, so that by the mid-thirteenth century the Rushton lands extended upstream from the grange site on the Hodder to include the whole of the upper Hodder basin as far as the watershed with the Wenning.

Meanwhile the descendants of the first Anglian colonisers were patiently clearing forest and scrub from the hillslopes around their villages and turning the ground to tillage. In this way the frontier of cultivation advanced outwards from the original clearances on to the higher, often more difficult, ground along the moorland margins. The building of new farms accompanied this advance into the wilderness. The development of this new settlement is usually difficult to reconstruct because it took place very gradually, each farmer clearing only a few acres during his entire lifetime, and the process went almost wholly unrecorded. Nevertheless by studying the form of place-names and noting the dates of their earliest appearance in records, much can be learned about these woodland clearances. Names ending in -*ley* and -*hurst* invariably indicate reclamation from a wooded area, while -*shaw* names usually show the existence of a former copse. Names ending in -*den* or -*dene* are usually derived from *denu* meaning valley. Field names containing *stubbins* indicate ground which was stubbed (i.e. the tree roots cleared) for cultivation, while a *ridding* field name means an enclosure from woodland or moorland waste. Along the Yorkshire Calder, *royd*, was a common variant of *ridding*. *Royd* names are thus frequent on the slopes above the Calder valley as at Hebden Royd, Mytholmroyd, Netheroyd, Boothroyd and Kebroyd.

In other areas the feudal lords of the Pennines discouraged or even prohibited further clearance and settlement, particularly in the forests and chases, for these were domains set aside for the lord's sport. By the twelfth century many such forests had been established in England. The largest were the royal forests, which reached their greatest extent during the reign of Henry II, but there were also many seignorial forests, the private chases of individual lords, and the Pennine forests were of this type. The Pennines, with their sharp juxtaposition of wooded valleys and wild craggy moorlands, provided fine hunting ground for the lords of England's northern marches.

Much of the Honour of Clitheroe comprised forest; and the Lacy earls of Lincoln, lords of the Honour, had chases in Bowland, Accrington, Rossendale, Pendle and Trawden. The largest of these chases was Bowland, corresponding in area on the present-day map to the townships of Bowland Forest High, Bowland Forest Low, and Bowland-with-Leagram. Hunting in Bowland was organised from a lodge at Whitewell on the Hodder (Fig 8). The chase was supervised for its lord by his Master Forester who was helped by assistant foresters, one for each ward or division of the chase. Their function was the guardianship and protection of the deer, and the apprehension of poachers. These and other malefactors were brought before the lord's forest or woodmote court held regularly at Whitewell (Chapter 5).

The history of Bowland Forest is interesting in that it casts light on the extent of forests in very early times, before written records of their limits were made. Examination of its boundaries and the extent of the jurisdiction of its courts shows that the Forest was probably originally bigger than its extant boundaries suggest. The Master Forester is known to have collected a traditional levy called a *puture* rent from all Forest dwellers. In the fourteenth century putures were collected not merely

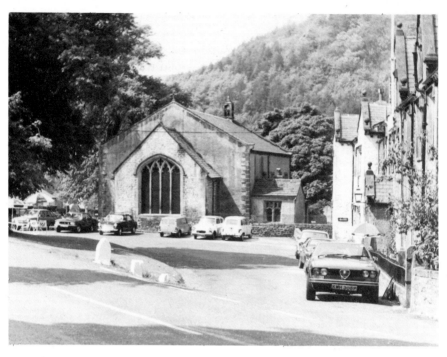

8    Whitewell was a hunting lodge in the medieval Forest of Bowland and the seat of its manorial courts. The wayside chapel-of-ease dates from the fifteenth century.

from the Forest, but also from several villages adjoining it although outside its boundaries. The explanation seems to be that in pre-Conquest times, the jurisdiction of Bowland Forest extended beyond its fourteenth century boundaries to include the whole of the Hodder basin and adjoining villages along the Ribble. In later times the Forest was cut back by village expansion to the area of the three Forest townships mentioned above. Bolton-by-Bowland, a village now six miles from the later Forest boundary, was so named since in pre-Conquest times it would have stood on the very edge of the Forest. Other Pennine forests experienced similar contraction in response to the expansion of settlement within their boundaries.

Forests were not always left aside solely as hunting grounds. By the middle of the thirteenth century some forest lords were trying to devise ways of making their chases produce an economic return. They turned to livestock rearing, using their valley and moorland wastes as pasture for herds of long-horned, shaggy, black-haired cattle. Rearing was carried out from domainal farms called vaccaries. These were crude, timber-built structures with thatched roofs, the homes of old forest families obliged to take their lord's cattle for pasturage. For most of the year the hardy cattle were allowed to roam at will over the bleak moorlands and were brought down to the vaccary only during bad weather. The vaccary enterprises developed to considerable proportions, for no fewer than 2,500 beasts were kept over the winters of both 1295-6 and 1304-5 in the Lacy chases of Accrington, Pendle, Trawden, and Rossendale. In Rossendale there were eleven vaccaries along the narrow, twisting Irwell valley east of Haslingden and its tributaries extending northwards towards the Calder-Irwell watershed. The later industrial towns and villages of Rawtenstall, Crawshaw Booth, Goodshaw and Bacup all began life as vaccaries of the Lacy earls of Lincoln.

The conversion of Forests to cattle-rearing grounds encouraged the restriction of deer to enclosures or deer parks where they could breed in safety but could be released into the Forest for the chase as required. In the Forest of Sowerby along the Yorkshire Calder there was a deer park at Erringden, and there were others at Musbury in Rossendale and at Leagram and Radholme in Bowland. Leagram Park, which lay just to the east of Chipping, was created about 1340. It was surrounded by a ditch some 4ft deep and 8ft wide with the earth thrown up on the outer side to form a bank. The bank was surmounted by a fence of stakes or 'pales' of split oak, on either side of which were rows of thorns. Gaps in the fence allowed the deer to come and go at will. The park was supervised from a lodge, the site of which is now occupied by Leagram Hall. The farm names *Park Gate* and *Pale Farm* recall this period in Leagram's history.

Vaccary farming was in decline by the later fourteenth century for the depressed economic conditions of the time made commercial cattle rearing unprofitable and the lords began to let their vaccaries to tenants for rent. From this time onwards the vaccaries were broken down into smaller but more numerous holdings, thus initiating the growth of new forest communities. The fourteenth and fifteenth centuries were times of general economic decline and social disorder; low grain prices caused the abandonment of cultivated lands in north and west Lancashire; border raids by the Scots sometimes penetrated as far south as Ribblesdale, leaving havoc and devastation in their trail; and the Wars of the Roses divided allegiances and encouraged armed uprisings, widespread civil disorder, and administrative corruption. All these troubles promoted uncertainty and insecurity.

Yet despite these problems, the countryside continued to fill up with people and trade flourished. The system of regular markets and fairs established under the Normans continued to develop. The broad, long market square at Skipton indicates the scale of the commerce which developed there under the protection of the castle walls. Skipton quickly developed as a market centre of great importance because it served the extensive, well-settled Craven lowlands, as it does today. There were, however, many other smaller market centres serving localised trading areas; for example the name of the village of *Chipping* indicates a medieval market centre. Such a market must have grown up to serve the needs of the new farms that in the eleventh and twelfth centuries were colonising the lower slopes of Bowland. There is no longer a market at Chipping; but the central Pennines have more villages like Chipping where in medieval times small groups of local farmers, craftsmen and labourers gathered once weekly to exchange their produce, sell their labour, and meet their neighbours.

**Selected further reading;**
E. Ekwall, *The Place-Names of Lancashire*, Manchester, 1922 (reprinted E.P. Publishing, 1972)
F. and H.W. Elgee, *The Archaeology of Yorkshire*, Methuen, 1933 (reprinted S.R Publishers, 1971)
R.C. Shaw, *The Royal Forest of Lancaster*, Preston, 1956
G.H. Tupling, 'The Pre-Reformation Parishes and Chapelries of Lancashire', *Transactions of the Lancashire & Cheshire Antiquarian Society*, vol 67 (1957)
F.T. Wainwright (ed H.P.R. Finberg), *Scandinavian England*, Phillimore, 1975

# 3 Moorland Colonisers and Cloth Makers 1450-1770

Pendle Forest is a pleasant rural corner of east Lancashire occupying the slopes between the industrialised valley of Pendle Water and the towering summit of Pendle Hill. The highest parts of Pendle Forest are bleak moorland, the lowest parts urban sprawl; between the two there is a district of hamlets, scattered farms, and twisting country lanes. Pendle Forest is well known as the haunt of a number of women hung for witchcraft after trial at Lancaster castle in 1612. From this event, romanticised in the novels of Harrison Ainsworth and Robert O'Neill, has developed the popular image of seventeenth century Pendle as a district of black crags, swirling mists, and old crones 'sparing no man with fearful execrable cures', a place where no man 'neither his wife, children, goods or cattle could be secure or free from danger.'

Historical records however paint a rather different picture of Pendle Forest. Poverty, ignorance, and superstition, the foundations of witchcraft, were indeed present, but there were few places in seventeenth century England from which they were completely absent. Pendle was a community dominated not by witches but by thriving small farmers who during the course of the Tudor and Stuart centuries transformed themselves from peasants into yeomen on the proceeds of their corn, milk and wool. They augmented their income from the land by weaving plain narrow cloths in their new, handsome, stone-built farmhouses, and these dwellings today form one of the most pleasing features of the Pendle scene.

The population of Pendle Forest grew rapidly in the sixteenth and early seventeenth centuries, a sure sign of rising prosperity. This growth is reflected in the swelling in size of the old forest hamlets. The hamlet of Barley Booth had only nine homesteads in 1507 and ten in 1608, but had twenty-six by 1662. Goldshaw Booth had twelve households in 1507, fifteen in 1608, and forty-three in 1662. In Roughlee Booth the corresponding figures were thirteen, twenty-three, and thirty-three. By the Restoration the total population of the Forest had grown to about 1,400 or around three times the size of the population of a century and a half earlier.

The growth of Pendle was typical of the development of Pennine communities in the Tudor and Stuart eras. Throughout the central Pennines from Wyresdale to Holmfirth a new prosperity was changing the way of life of the inhabitants and transforming the features of the landscape. A fundamental redistribution of population took place as settlement spread to the higher valleys and moorland slopes, areas hitherto sparsely inhabited. Isolated hillside farmsteads became transformed into clusters of dwellings, while hamlets grew into villages. The hillsides took on a new look as lines of low hedges and stone walls carved them up into small fields and the rough moorland grasses gave way to sown pastures. The landscape became dotted with new stone-built cottages and farms, outside each of which stood the tenter or cloth drying frame, a visible symbol of the new prosperity.

Land was the key to the region's new wealth and populousness. Until the sixteenth century the moors had been in the hands of great lords who discouraged new settlers in order to preserve these lands as chases or hunting grounds. The largest landowner in the central Pennines was the Crown, which owned several chases among its extensive lands in the region, but by the sixteenth century the Crown was taking a different view of its empty moorlands, seeing their value not in terms of the number of deer that might be hunted there during a season but rather of the income the lands might bring if they could be let for farming. The Tudor and early Stuart monarchs therefore encouraged the colonisation of their moorlands in order to bring them new revenue.

At the same time the market for land seems to have greatly increased as a consequence of sustained population growth. There appears also to have been a steady influx of new families into the region, possibly wanderers who could find no land for settlement in more densely populated parts of England. Encouraged by the new attitude of the Crown a steady stream of poor farmers began to carve new holdings out of the Pennine fringes. Many were squatters with no entitlement to the land they occupied, but far from resisting their colonisation the Crown went out of its way to legalise their occupation by nominal fines in its manorial courts.

The moorlands of east Lancashire provide an illustration of how this invasion of empty lands came about. In 1507 Henry VII abolished the forest laws relating to the chases of Bowland, Accrington, Rossendale, Pendle, and Trawden. Freed of restrictions on settlement, the few old-established forest families began to enlarge the fields around their

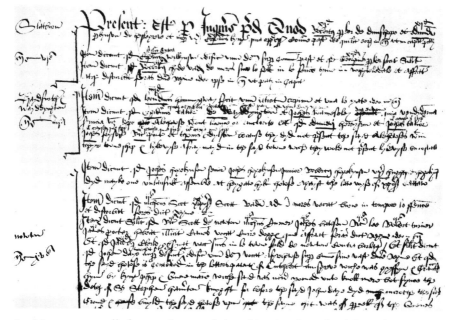

9 Manor court rolls frequently record the taking in of new land from the waste. This Slaidburn manor court roll of 1561 records, among many other matters, encroachments on the common wastes of Slaidburn and Newton.

homesteads from the wasteland. As each family developed more branches generation by generation, properties were divided up within the family into ever smaller holdings. Families from outside swelled the growing communities establishing new colonies or offshoots of existing settlements. A further boost to settlement in east Lancashire came in 1608 when James I conferred security of tenure on the region's many copyholders. As part of the agreement between the Crown and its tenants the copyholders were allowed to enclose large tracts of moorland at very advantageous rents. The result was that almost every community grew considerably during the period between 1507 and the Restoration. Slaidburn in Bowland grew from some fifty-six households in 1539 to ninety-eight in 1664; Trawden Forest had only twenty-five households in 1527 but thirty-nine in 1662, while Colne township grew from fifty-one to seventy-four households and Rawtenstall from four to twenty-one over the same period.

This retreat of the Pennine moorland fringes came about through gradual encroachment on the wastes by the individual farmer reclaiming perhaps only one or two acres a year, but during a lifetime of work adding three or four new fields to his farm. In some cases an enterprising

31

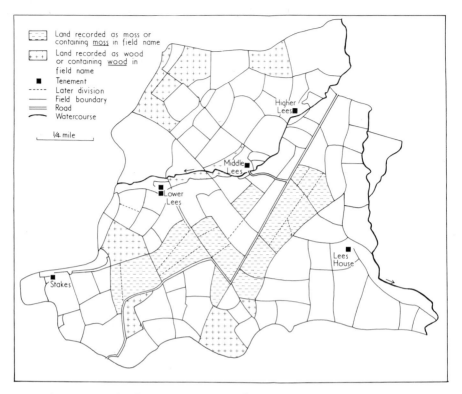

Legend:
- Land recorded as moss or containing moss in field name
- Land recorded as wood or containing wood in field name
- ■ Tenement
- ----- Later division
- —— Field boundary
- ═══ Road
- —— Watercourse

¼ mile

Higher Lees■

Middle■ Lees

■Lower Lees

Lees House■

■Stakes

10  The Lees, Bowland Forest, 1652, soon after its reclamation and enclosure. Field names reflect the area's former wooded and marshy character.

villager might buy from his farmer neighbours a consolidated block of new enclosures on which he would build a new farmstead. In this way the frontier of settlement gradually advanced up the moorland slopes. Although much of this colonisation went unrecorded, evidence of encroachments occasionally survives in manor records. Where many encroachments in a locality are recorded, it may be possible to piece the references together in chronological sequence and recreate on a map the order in which new farms were created from the wilderness.

Such is the case in a district called the Lees on the slopes of the Hodder valley in Bowland Forest (Fig 10). In the early sixteenth century the Lees was a partly wooded, partly marshy tract used for rough grazing. From the middle of the sixteenth century this ground was colonised and steadily enclosed, and the date of origin of certain farms can be traced. In 1567 Thomas Turner is recorded as having felled timber to build a house. This was probably Higher Lees, occupied in 1652 by his descendant, another Thomas Turner. Lower Lees, occupied in 1652 by Robert

Parker, was built by his father Alexander Parker in 1596. The same Alexander Parker in 1621 is recorded as having destroyed two acres of woodland. He gave Henry Robinson enough of this timber to build a cottage which was occupied by Robinson or his descendant of the same name in 1652. As these new farmsteads were built, so the woodland wastes around them were gradually cleared. Near Stakes Farm eight acres of woodland were enclosed in 1603 and a further three acres in 1621. In 1613 Thomas Turner stubbed (ie pulled up by the roots) fourteen acres of woodland, while further enclosures were made by the Rathmell family of Lower Lees in 1622 and 1631.

These enclosures were the work of individual farmers, but in some cases enclosures were made by entire communities who bargained with their landlords as a single party to determine the terms of enclosure. In 1586 the township of Grindleton in the Ribble valley petitioned the Crown, its landlord, to be allowed to enclose a moorland called Smalden used at that time by the township as a common pasture. For some years the Grindleton villagers had been anxiously watching the progress of enclosure by their neighbours in Bolton-by-Bowland of moors called West Moor and Holden Bank which adjoined Smalden. They complained to the Crown that since the Bolton men had made these 'improvements', reducing in size their own area of common pasture, they had taken to pasturing their stock on Smalden instead. An equally important problem was that

> the said town of Grindleton is of late greatly increased in buildings and dwelling houses and thereby much more populated than heretofore it hath been, by reason whereof the ancient grounds used and employed to pasture, meadow, and tillage, are in no sort able and sufficient to maintain our said freeholders and copyholders whereby much poverty doth daily increase amongst them and is more and more like to do if some good provision be not had and foreseen in time…

and that this situation could only be alleviated by enclosure of Smalden. The Crown readily agreed, and as a result 364 acres of Smalden were divided among sixty-two Grindleton copyholders the following year. However a dispute broke out between Grindleton and commoners from Sawley who also claimed common rights on Smalden, and it was some years before the enclosure of the moor was completed.

Some larger moorland tracts were divided not merely between the people of one community but between the inhabitants of several neighbouring communities. Another example from the Grindleton district illustrates this. A mile off the road between Grindleton and Slaidburn lies a farm called Champion. The name was originally applied not merely to this farm but to the 2,400 acre tract of moorland of which the farm occupies a small portion. The name is derived from the Norman

French *campagne*, meaning open field or land. In medieval times all the villages adjoining Champion had the right to pasture livestock there. When Champion was enclosed soon after 1622, the apportionment of the common between the village reflected these ancient pasturing rights. Slaidburn acquired 915 acres from Champion, Grindleton gained 610 acres, and Chatburn 327 acres, the remaining land being divided between four smaller communities. The number of acres allotted to each village was roughly in proportion to the number of livestock it had previously grazed on the common. Over the following half century the farmers who gained these allotments and their descendants built twenty-three new farmsteads on Champion. Had not one farm taken over the name of the old common, the name itself might have been lost from the district for ever.

The colonisation of the moorlands and the growing populousness of Pennine villages meant that many churches became too small for their enlarged congregations. It is not surprising therefore that the period saw the foundation of new parishes and chapelries, particularly in outlying districts in which population growth was very rapid. Until the sixteenth century the twenty-five townships of Halifax parish had been served only by the mother church and chapels at Heptonstall and Elland. During this century new chapels were established at Sowerby, at Illingworth for Ovenden township, at Luddenden for Midgley and Warley and at Coley to serve the three townships of Shelf, North-owram, and Hipperholme. In Rossendale new chapels were founded at Newchurch in 1511 and at Goodshaw in 1540. Pennine Lancashire also has another Newchurch—that in Pendle, founded around 1529. Newchurch-in-Pendle today is a quiet country hamlet; by contrast the sister church in Rossendale overlooks the remains of the tide of in-dustrialism that engulfed the upper Irwell valley in subsequent centuries.

Most new farms created out of the Pennine hillsides were small and poor. Their occupiers thrived not by tilling the sterile soils but by keeping small flocks of sheep which they could pasture on the still unappropriated higher moorlands. This sheep herding soon became the basis of another, more important means of livelihood. The cold wet Pennine winters offered little scope for work outdoors, and from the earliest times the upland farmers of Lancashire and Yorkshire had resorted to the spinning wheel and loom to supplement their income from the land. During the sixteenth and seventeenth centuries textile manufacture grew very quickly among the many new small farmers and cottagers. According to Rossendale's historian, G. H. Tupling, 'settlers were attracted not so much by the prospect of becoming well-to-do farmers, as by the mere facility with which land might be enclosed or acquired in order to set up a homestead'. For many such settlers the small-holding was simply a means to enable them to keep a cow or two and a few sheep; it was cloth manufacture which provided them with the most important part of their living.

By the seventeenth century the Pennine moors were becoming well covered with the flocks of hardy sheep which provided the raw material for the cloth industry. We can envisage that the industry originated with the farmer's wife spinning the wool into a thread which her husband would weave into a piece of cloth on his primitive narrow loom in his spare time. The weaver would soon find that he needed several spinners to keep him fully supplied with yarn, and also the help of other women and children for operations such as combing or carding. Consequently the entire family and neighbours would become employed in the business, and a well-lighted room in the cottage would be transformed into a small workshop containing a loom, two or three spinning wheels, and carding or combing tools (Fig 11). In this way there developed the 'domestic' system of textile manufacture which provided the staple

11  Simple handlooms such as this could be found in most Pennine households in pre-industrial times and provided an additional income for many poorer farmers.

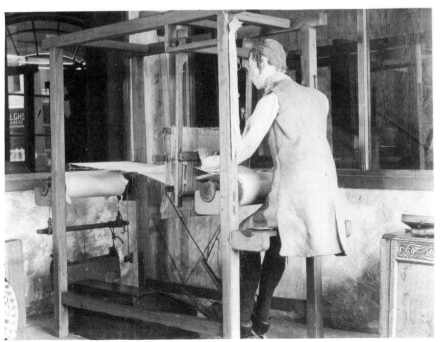

means of livelihood in the Pennines for two centuries.

Cloth manufacture became especially widespread along the flanks of the main Pennine axis south of the Ribble and Aire where farming land was poor and squatting had broken up the hillsides into many small holdings. It was less common in Bowland and Craven, but there were few parts of the Pennines which did not have a fair sprinkling of domestic weavers. In Lancashire the industry grew particularly quickly in Rossendale and the hills around Bury and Rochdale. Yates' map of Lancashire, published in 1786, depicts the district around Rochdale in the ancient townships of Spotland, Castleton, and Butterworth thick with cottages and hamlets, all lying close to tracks and roads focusing upon this market town (Fig 12). In Yorkshire the Calder valley and its tributaries between Todmorden and Halifax, and the Colne valley above Huddersfield and across into Saddleworth became especially important. The products of the trade were varied. Coarse heavy *friezes* and woollen *cottons* were widespread, as were the lighter and better quality *kerseys*. As the industry grew, product specialisation developed.

12 Yates' map of Lancashire (1786) is the earliest large-scale printed map to show the whole of the county. Besides settlements and roads, the map also depicts minor features such as mills, coal pits, chapels, milestones, and gentlemen's seats. This extract reveals that the district around Rochdale was closely settled with many hamlets and cottages, only the high moorland wastes remaining unpopulated.

By the eighteenth century imported vegetable cotton was finding its way into Lancashire so that the district between Blackburn and Bury began to manufacture *fustians*, fabrics of cotton weft and linen or woollen warp. Worsted manufacture rose to predominance along Airedale around Keighley, Bingley, and Bradford.

The organisation of cloth manufacture soon acquired considerable complexity. Some enterprising weavers began to employ other weavers in their workshops or to put out work to weavers and spinners elsewhere. In this way a class of clothiers grew up. In the sixteenth century they were men of small means, unable

> to keep a horse to carry wools nor yet to buy much wool at once, but hath ever used only to repair to the town of Halifax and some other nigh thereto,

13   Greenwood Lee, Hebden Bridge. This former merchant clothier's house is dated 1712. The left-hand gable conceals the site of a waterwheel used to drive weaving machinery. The house stands on an old packhorse route from Colne to Heptonstall.

and there to buy upon the wooldriver some a stone, some two, some three or four and to carry the same to their houses, some three, four, five, and six miles off, upon their heads and backs.

By the eighteenth century, these clothiers were men of substance. W. Bennett provides some details of the activities of a clothier named Parker of Carr Hall in Nelson. He had cloth depots at Carr Hall and at Bank Fold near Haslingden and dealt in linen, wool, cotton, and stocking yarn. He employed several weavers, spinners, and dyers. One weaver who worked for Parker was William Cook, who in the years around 1723 took from Parker some 1,100 lb of yarn for making up into cloth and supplied him with 800 lb of finished cloth in 127 pieces. Parker sent the cloth out for dyeing; between January and July 1723 he had nearly 200 lb of cloth dyed. He sold the finished products at Halifax, Colne, and Kildwick markets. At Colne and certain other market towns the cloth traders met in specialised premises called cloth halls; the Heptonstall Cloth Hall, which still stands, flourished between about 1500 and 1700 before it was superseded by the larger market at Halifax.

The old market towns of the Pennines also began to contribute their share to the growing industry. Since medieval times Burnley, Colne, Rochdale, and Halifax had been centres for fulling, one of the final stages in cloth production in which grease is removed from the cloth by pounding it under water. The farmer-weavers of the surrounding countryside had long been accustomed to sending their pieces of cloth to the fulling mills of these towns. It is hardly surprising therefore that it was these same towns which became focal points for cloth manufacture. They housed many small weavers such as Edward Butterworth of Rochdale, who died in 1598 leaving a loom, two spinning wheels, wool cards and combs, as well as some cows and crops. John Broxoppe of Blackburn, who died in 1582, left no livestock and relied entirely on weaving for a living, leaving a loom 'to weave woollen cloth on' and a store of wool and yarn. Some larger towns soon began to stand out as centres of trade in wool and finished cloth. Rochdale, which had at least six fulling mills in 1626, became the focal point of the trade in Pennine Lancashire and the headquarters of the many clothiers and middlemen who organised the 'putting out' system in the surrounding districts. Halifax and Leeds drew in the produce of the industry on the Yorkshire side. Defoe, in his *Tour through the Whole Island of Great Britain* (1726), described the Leeds cloth market as 'a prodigy of its kind, and is not to be equalled in the world.' He was hardly less impressed by the commercial importance of Halifax, and his account of the town dwells particularly on the severity of the local laws devised for the protection of the cloth trade. Until 1650 cloth stealers were liable to execution at the Halifax gibbet, a guillotine-like scaffold which stood on a hillside above the town and gained a fearsome reputation throughout Yorkshire. Clothiers from Halifax frequently put out wool to weavers in villages as far away as Austwick and Wigglesworth in Craven, where old milestones sometimes give distances to Halifax.

By the middle of the eighteenth century Halifax had established clear predominance over other Pennine cloth markets. In 1779 its new cloth market building, the Piece Hall, was opened, an open rectangle of some ten thousand square yards surrounded by a two-storey colonnade with Italian columns and containing 315 rooms, each occupied by a cloth manufacturer. Business was transacted between ten and twelve o'clock each Saturday morning, smaller cloth makers selling their one or two pieces in the open area. A directory of the Hall for 1787 shows that cloth makers came not just from the Halifax area but from as far afield as Pendle, Burnley, and Skipton. Cloth was sold not merely to local merchants but to buyers from all over the kingdom and to agents acting for continental buyers. The Piece Hall is one of the most important architectural monuments of the Pennines and reflects the zenith of the pre-factory wool trade.

14 Mount Cross stands high on the moors between Burnley and Hebden Bridge and overlooks the Cliviger gorge. Stone crosses helped to guide travellers and packhorse trains in bad weather.

The trade in cloth and wool between town and country, between woolstapler, clothier, and weaver, gave rise to another class of merchant, a middleman variously called a chapman, brogger, or jagger. He lived by distributing wool to the many scattered weavers and clothiers and collecting their finished cloth pieces for sale in cloth markets throughout England. He carried his produce not on carts but on long trains of packhorses using paved tracks called causeways which avoided the valley floors and ran straight across the moorland plateaux to join together the hillside communities which provided the chapman's stock-in-trade. Some of these causeways have now become surfaced roads, such as the Long Causeway between Burnley and Heptonstall which avoids the low route through Cliviger and instead crosses the main Pennine watershed by the high plateau of Black Hameldon. Others have degenerated into rarely used footpaths or have disappeared from the map altogether, such as the ancient road from Newchurch-in-Rossendale to Burnley via Gambleside. Yet some paved causeways remain as they were two centuries ago, their causeys or flags overgrown but their alignments clearly visible (Chapter 10). Many old packhorse routes have the remains of stone crosses at points along their lengths (Fig 14). There are some forty sites of such crosses in the central Pennines. They may have served to mark the way in bad weather and were perhaps used as well known meeting places for the moorland communities.

In the turbulent religious and political climate of the period, hilltop gatherings were not infrequent. Henry VIII's dissolution of the monasteries in 1536 provoked widespread unrest in the north of England where the old abbeys had fulfilled a useful social role through their alms and good works. In Craven and Bowland resistance to the suppression of Sawley and Whalley culminated in an armed gathering by the ancient cross at Monubent Moor near Bolton-by-Bowland, and although the rebellion was suppressed and the abbeys reduced to ruins, recusancy or adherence to the Catholic faith long remained strong in the region. A century later armed gatherings returned to the Pennines when the war between King and Parliament once again divided society. Yet another century later further moorland meetings announced the emergence of nonconformity from its furtive existence in converted houses to become the religion of the new factory working classes. In 1766 John Wesley preached at Widdop on the road between Nelson and Heptonstall from a rock still called Wesley's Pulpit, and from this and many other mass gatherings grew the chapels which were to become a dominant feature of the Pennine landscape in the following century.

As the prosperity of Pennine farmers and cloth makers grew, so their living styles began to change likewise. The smallholder of Tudor times had been content to live in a rough one-storey cottage with stone and clay walls and a rush thatched roof. The clothiers, wealthier weavers and farmers of a century later built themselves substantial stone houses of two storeys with higher ceilings and stone flagged roofs. The windows of these houses are divided into narrow lights by vertical stone mullions, and the doorways often bear an ornate lintel containing the date of building and the initials of the builder, usually its first occupier. One room in these houses often has a noticeably larger mullioned window to let in more light; this was the workroom where the weavers sat at their looms. The houses were built from local stone to withstand Pennine weather and were designed by their occupiers for a Pennine way of life; they represent a period in the history of the central Pennines when man and his physical surroundings were closely matched to each other.

Defoe, in his journey through west Yorkshire in the 1720s sensed this relationship between man and the land. His account of his descent from Blackstone Edge along the road to Sowerby Bridge and Halifax captures vividly the wild mountainous quality of this part of the Pennines, a country of blinding snow storms and deep precipices. Yet he observed the 'bounty of nature to this otherwise frightful country' in providing frequent coal seams and running water for the cloth manufacture. He noted the many dispersed cottages and workshops along the hillsides and the tenter frames on which the cloth was stretched to dry. He also noticed the diligence of the inhabitants, 'all employed upon the manufacture, and all seeming to have sufficient business.' It was this industriousness that was to provide the basis for the great changes in the Pennine scene yet to come.

**Selected further reading**:

W. Bennett, *The History of Burnley*, Vols 2 & 3, Burnley 1947-8

M. Brigg, 'The Forest of Pendle in the Seventeenth Century', *Transactions of the Lancashire and Cheshire Historic Society*, vol 114 (1963), 115 (1964)

D. Defoe, *Tour Through the Whole Island of Great Britain*, Dent, Everyman ed, 1962

T. W. Hanson, *The Story of Old Halifax*, Halifax, 1920 (reprinted S.R. Publishers, 1968)

N. Lowe, 'The Lancashire Textile Industry in the Sixteenth Century', *Chetham Society*, 3rd ser, vol 20 (1972)

G. H. Tupling, *The Economic History of Rossendale*, Manchester, 1927

# 4 The Growth of Industries And Towns 1770-1900

In Exchange Street, Blackburn, there is a small museum which houses a collection of the early textile machinery on which the former prosperity of the Pennine textile districts was built. The machines are exhibited not in isolation but in reconstructions of the surroundings in which they might have been found when working. Here, within a few paces of each other, can be seen the transition from the domestic textile industry, the rise of which was described in the last chapter, to the factory system of production which was to bring such widespread changes to the area's way of life and its landscape.

The transition was spread over a century but the most far-reaching changes were compressed into little more than a generation. It began in a modest way when John Kay, a Bury reed-maker, in 1733 patented a device that replaced the hand operation of the shuttle across the weaver's loom by a mechanical motion, speeding up the weaving action and making it more accurate. Although Kay met a lot of opposition to his 'flying shuttle' and gained little personal benefit from it, the device nevertheless spread very quickly and was soon in general use throughout the textile districts.

Each weaver had always required several spinners to supply him with yarn, but the acceleration of weaving now created a general yarn shortage. Enterprising clothiers therefore turned their attention to the problem of increasing the yarn supply. Between 1738 and 1758 John Wyatt and Lewis Paul of Sutton Coldfield, Warwickshire, experimented with mechanical spinning devices, but it fell to an Oswald-twistle weaver, James Hargreaves, to invent the first spinning machine around 1768. He never promoted his 'jenny' commercially and it was overshadowed by another machine invented quite independently. This was the mechanical superior 'water frame' of Richard Arkwright, a Preston barber whose entrepreneurial ability ensured its rapid acceptance. The most effective and widely used spinning device however was the 'mule' invented in 1779 by Samuel Crompton, a poor spinner, who lived in the then tenemented old mansion of Hall i'th Wood, near Bolton, and who is reputed to have raised the money necessary for buying the tools to build his machine by playing the fiddle at Bolton theatre (Fig 15). The mule combined the principles of jenny and water frame and became the standard form of spinning machine used in the textile mills until after 1870. Improvements in spinning were accompanied by the mechanisation of the preliminary processes of carding and scribbling, so that by 1820 the technology of the spinning and associated trades had been changed beyond recognition from half a century earlier.

These technical innovations did not lead immediately to changes in the landscape. They were applied first within the homes and workshops of the many artisans and clothiers whose premises could be extended to contain the new, larger machinery. But it soon became apparent that the new machines could not operate efficiently without some form of additional power and that they could function more

15   Samuel Crompton 'inventing' his Spinning Mule. He lived at Hall i' th' Wood, Bolton, for much of his life.

profitably not in the home but in large workshops or mills where several machines could be accommodated under one roof. From about 1780 onwards therefore small water-powered mills became increasingly common in the Pennine valleys, particularly in Lancashire. The adoption of power spinning in the eastern Pennine districts was slower, although power carding was soon established there.

Dr Tupling, in his classic study of the economic history of Rossendale, traced in detail the impact of the new machinery on the economy of the upper Irwell region and the transformation of the industry's organisation from a domestic to a factory system. Like many central Pennine districts, eighteenth century Rossendale was a community of many dispersed farms and loosely-knit hamlets such as Tunstead, Holden, Bacup, and Balladen, supported by a dual economy of farming and hand-made woollen textiles. The many moorland streams however provided a diversity of mill sites, and by the 1780s landowners were becoming eager to sell or let their water rights to prospective entrepreneurs. Thus in 1788 an advertisement in the *Manchester Mercury* offered for sale a farm at Cowpe, which on account of its fine stream was described as 'a very proper place for erecting a cotton or woollen engine therein'. Carding mills were the first to become common, sometimes utilising old corn

16    Mills in Rossendale, c1840. Few suitable sites were not utilised. By this time cotton manufactures had largely superseded woollen goods.

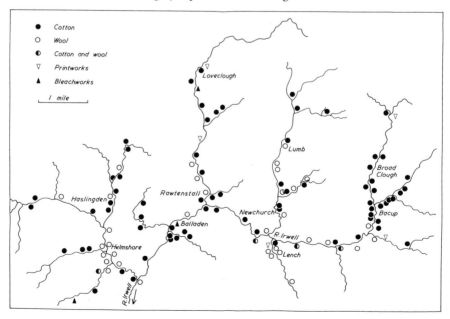

mill premises, and by 1825 there were eleven in Bacup alone. Spinning and fulling mills and dyeworks followed, so that by the 1840s there were few streams which did not support a string of mills and dyehouses (Fig 16).

By the early nineteenth century all-cotton goods were growing in importance in the Rossendale textile trade, leading eventually to the almost total ousting of wool. Since cotton thread could be spun much more easily than wool on the new machinery, its adoption accelerated the introduction of machines and the spread of spinning mills. These early mills were quite small; one at Ewood Bridge was stated to be 25 yd long, 13 yd wide, four storeys high, and to accommodate 4,000 spindles, besides carding and other machinery. Not all of these early factories survived this first stage of industrialisation; many were long ago demolished and their foundations are now overgrown.

Until 1840 weaving in Rossendale remained firmly in the hands of the many small weavers who plied their trade in workshops or spare rooms in their own homes. Indeed, the rapid growth in yarn output as a result of mechanisation meant that for many years hand loom weavers were in great demand and the trade became lucrative. At this time many cottages were built with a spare room to house the weaving machinery. In other Pennine districts this room was most commonly on the first or second floor, but in Rossendale a mixture of upper floor, ground floor, and basement loomshops were built. Many weavers were wholly self-employed, whereas others worked for small masters who employed a dozen or so men in loomshops containing three or four looms. Coarse calicoes were the most common product and were either sold locally or found their way to the Manchester market.

Haslingden Grane is an outlying and now deserted part of Rossendale, but in the early nineteenth century it was a flourishing weaving community comprising many scattered farms and 'folds' or clusters of cottages. From these isolated dwellings weavers regularly carried their cloth into Haslingden on their donkeys, returning with warps and wefts of yarn from the spinning mills. From Haslingden itself one cotton master who owned three looms in his cottage in Pleasant Street frequently carried his finished pieces of shirtings or 'bump' fabrics all the way on his back to the Manchester warehouses. Sometimes he made use of the stagecoach, which became known as the 'bump' coach, since it was used mainly by these small manufacturers. Some outlying weavers were visited by pedlars who served on foot an area of some fifteen or twenty miles around Haslingden and could be seen treading the moorland tracks with pack and yardstick well into the 1850s.

As the nineteenth century progressed another technical innovation wrought further widespread changes in the economic geography of Rossendale. The steam engine, first applied to spinning machinery in

Nottinghamshire in 1775, was at work in the Pennine textile districts by 1790. It was however slow to supersede water power for at first it was less reliable and prodigal of fuel. Nevertheless steam engines could power bigger mills than most water wheels and were less restricted in choice of site. The industry responded by abandoning smaller mills and convertings others to steam. Since coal was expensive to transport new mills were most frequently built in the more accessible lower valleys. Another important application of the new steam power was to weaving. As early as 1786 Edmund Cartwright patented a power loom, but its adoption was slow at first. Power weaving made its first appearance in Rossendale with the erection of the Rawtenstall Higher Mill, started by the Whitehead brothers in 1822. Anti-power loom riots in 1826 temporarily retarded the development of power weaving, but by 1840 it was claiming the lion's share of the weaving trade. Hand loom weaving was slow to die out completely in Rossendale and remained in the area until 1880. Its disappearance completed the transformation of the area from one dependent for its livelihood on the land and the handicraft skills of its population to one dependent on machinery and factories.

The mechanisation of the clothing trade in Rossendale was repeated throughout the central Pennines. Few districts did not participate to some degree in this technical and organisational revolution. The new mills were most prolific in areas where the domestic clothing trade had been traditionally strong—the Huddersfield, Halifax, and Bradford areas of Yorkshire, and the Rossendale, Rochdale, and Calder valley regions of Lancashire. North of the Ribble the domestic trade had always been secondary to farming and the new industry never gained a real foothold. The mill system became established earliest in the Lancashire textile districts, only spreading later to the Yorkshire areas, and in remote localities around Huddersfield hand-loom weaving died very slowly. By 1840 product specialisation, already evident during the eighteenth century, was now well developed: worsteds were made in the Bradford area, woollens in the Huddersfield and Colne valley region spreading across the Pennines into Saddleworth and neighbouring Lancashire districts, and cotton products in the Lancashire Pennines. In the latter area weaving tended to dominate towns north of Rossendale, such as Blackburn and Burnley, while spinning was most widespread in the southern towns like Bolton, Bury, and Rochdale. The commercial centres of the old domestic trade, Rochdale and Halifax, were gradually superseded in importance by Manchester and Bradford respectively.

To keep pace with the new steam-powered industry, coal production grew rapidly. The proliferation of bleachworks and printworks further increased the demand for fuel. Coal seams occur widely, and coal pits were opened up wherever the mineral occurred close to the surface. There were a great many of these early pits but they were shallow, quickly exhausted, and soon abandoned. Their spoil heaps, now usually overgrown, give the landscape a distinctively hummocky appearance, and nearby there can often be found a Colliers' Row of cottages, a Coal Pit Lane along which the coals were hauled in carts down to a mill or bleachworks, or the remains of a tramway. The industry developed beyond this stage only where there were further seams at depth which could be economically exploited by the deeper mines made possible by improvements in mining technology. In 1850 a long string of collieries occupied the boundary between the Coal Measures and Millstone Grit of Yorkshire from Penistone northwards through Hepworth, Huddersfield, Halifax, and Denholme to Shipley. By 1895 however the number had greatly decreased and all were relatively small, each employing fewer than a hundred people; the impetus of the industry had shifted eastwards and southwards to the deeper, thicker seams around Wakefield and Barnsley.

More localised but more enduring in their effect on the landscape were the great stone quarries which by the mid-nineteenth century

17   Industrial landscape near Bacup, c1900. This landscape is dominated by sandstone quarries but coal workings and cotton mills also contribute to the industrial scene. Workers' cottages line much of the roadside between Stacksteads and Facit.

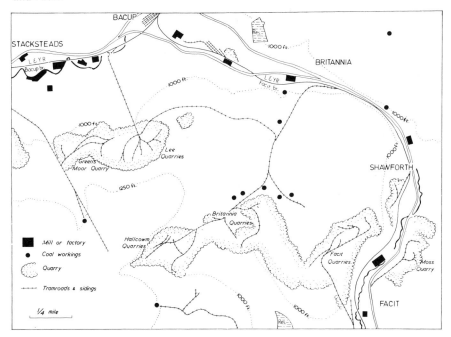

supplied the vastly increased demand for building stone as mills and new mill towns proliferated. Urban and industrial growth led to a great demand for stone not just for mills and houses but for the entire urban fabric of churches, chapels, town halls, public buildings, bridges, pavement flags, and stone setts for streets and roads. At Facit in Rossendale the Britannia quarries covered some two square miles and extracted stone from the valley to the summits of the moors three hundred feet above.

The greatly increased movement of materials and manufactured goods made necessary a revolution in means of transportation. During the later eighteenth and early nineteenth centuries turnpike trusts were established which improved many existing roads and in addition opened up a whole network of new ones. These new roads often followed different routes from their antecedents since they linked the growing mill communities along the valley bottoms, not the older villages and hamlets on the hillsides.

Horse power alone, however, could never hope to move the vast quantities of stone, coal, and corn required by the new mill towns. This was accomplished first by the canals, which arrived in the Pennines in 1773. The completion of the Rochdale Canal in 1804 was marked by the passage of the 50-ton seagoing vessel *Mayflower* all the way from Hull across the Pennines to Liverpool, and it was no wonder that people should have regarded with amazement the sight of a ship sailing through fields and woods.

The Rochdale Canal penetrated the Pennines by means of the boggy Walsden gorge, crossing the main divide at Summit, so-called since the canal builders could find no other name for this lonely spot. It initiated an era of crossing the Pennines by the lower routes in place of the high moorland trackways. Behind the canalmen came the railway navvies. In 1825 George Stephenson expressed interest in bringing the Pennines by a railway route from Manchester to Leeds using the Summit pass, but the necessary locomotive power and Act of Parliament were not available until a few years later. A plaque at Littleborough station commemorates the opening of the railway from Manchester to Summit in 1839; the Summit Tunnel and final stage of the railway were completed in 1841. A. F. Tait's engraving of the Littleborough end of the Summit Tunnel depicts an engineering work of monumental proportions and great visual power; and so the coming of the railway must have seemed to a population accustomed to the gentle pace of the stage waggon and packhorse train. By 1880 there were few Pennine valleys not served by the railway; it provided the region's most heavily used routes until the impact of the motor age, and its many yards and stations were the focal points around which economic life revolved. Today, when the Pennine railway age is mostly represented by tracks converted into bridleways, overgrown goods yards, and ruinous station platforms, it is becoming increasingly difficult to recall the stimulus to urban and industrial growth which rail transport provided.

The industrial growth and the transport revolution which accompanied it brought about a major redistribution both of population and major settlements. Until the nineteenth century, apart from old-established market towns, the population was widely scattered in many small villages, hamlets, and dispersed farms, mostly along the hillsides, leaving the marshy valley bottoms only sparsely populated, but with the growth of steam-powered mills requiring readily accessible coal and the development of valley-bottom canals and railways which could supply it, economic activity shifted to the valley floors together with the new factory-bound population. The growth of most valley mill villages and towns can be dated from this time. In Rossendale the old hillside settlements of Tunstead and Newchurch were superseded by Stack-steads and Waterfoot respectively. Haworth near Keighley is two quite distinct villages; the medieval village of the Brontë sisters high on the ridge between the Worth and Bridgehouse valleys, and the Victorian village almost two hundred feet below by the railway station.

This change in the settlement pattern was most noticeable along the valley of the Yorkshire Calder. Here, on benches high above the valley floor, a number of large villages had grown up in pre-industrial times. Each was the centre of a township which stretched from the moorland heights to the valley bottoms and each township was separated from its neighbours by tributary valleys. By the early nineteenth century however this pattern was changing. New valley floor settlements superseded the old hill villages, particularly at crossing points on the Calder. Sowerby was outgrown by Sowerby Bridge, Midgley by Mytholmroyd, and Rastrick by Brighouse, which at the time of Jeffreys' map of Yorkshire (1772) was merely a cluster of cottages around the Calder crossing. Further upstream an old packhorse road from Hepton-stall crossed the River Hebden just above its junction with the Calder; at this point Hebden Bridge grew up to become one of the principal towns of the Calder valley. Its growth has left Heptonstall poised high on the hillside like a museum of the pre-industrial era, overlooking, and puzzled by, the growth of the child it created.

By contrast, areas north of the Ribble experienced few of the changes which were bringing about the transformation of the landscape further south. Regions such as Bowland and Wyresdale had no coal resources and lay away from the main routes joining major towns. Consequently they were avoided by the builders of turnpikes, canals, and railways, and despite the existence of many suitable water mill sites the new textile masters preferred to develop the industry in districts where the domestic trade had been more deeply entrenched. Although some villages such as Chipping and Dolphinholme acquired mills, the old pattern of rural life continued largely undisturbed and society remained dominated by the long-established squirearchy. The Parker family of Browsholme maintained the rituals and traditions of the old Forest of Bowland while the Ribblesdale family of Gisburn introduced sika deer for hunting on their estate of Gisburn Park, kept a herd of wild white cattle, and planted hundreds of new oaks and other trees along the banks of the Ribble.

In districts like Bowland population remained static or even gently declined during the nineteenth century, whereas in the new industrial towns the rate of growth was nothing short of remarkable. The population of Bolton during the last quarter of the eighteenth century grew from 4,600 to 17,000, and from this to 168,000 by 1901. Burnley during the nineteenth century grew from 5,200 to 96,000, and Huddersfield from 7,000 to 95,000. These particular towns had all been flourishing market centres well before the Industrial Revolution, but other towns were entirely the product of the new factory era; Nelson grew up

18  Like all mill towns, Darwen grew rapidly during the nineteenth century, becoming a municipal borough in 1878. The town acquired steam trams in 1881 and the first electric tram ran in 1900.

around an inn of the same name and quickly absorbed the surrounding ancient township of Marsden. Neither Nelson nor its neighbour Brierfield are marked on the first edition Ordnance Survey one-inch map of 1858. Oldham in the mid-eighteenth century was a pleasant village clustered around a cross-roads on the ridge of Oldham Edge. By 1794 it had twelve cotton mills and a population of 10,000. From this it had spawned a population of 130,000 and 265 mills by 1888 and had become the world's greatest cotton spinning town. These massive rates of growth were accomplished partly by natural increase and partly by migration. The prospect of work attracted people not only from the countryside around the towns but also from Cumberland, Westmorland, Cheshire, Scotland, and Ireland. By the middle of the nineteenth century many once well populated rural townships of the Pennines were rapidly losing population as the hand loom weaving trade collapsed, and entire families moved to the growing mill towns in search of work. Rishworth at the head of Ryburn Dale had a population of 1,710 in 1841 but by 1901 this had slumped to 915.

As population grew the urban fabric expanded to contain it. In many towns the earliest industrial housing has been cleared to make way for tower blocks and council houses under post-war urban renewal schemes, leaving the post-1875 houses of the 'improved' standard as the chief survivors of the period of industrial prosperity. The spread of housing drew upon new material, organisational, and financial forces. Pre-industrial housing had been the work of the individual farmer or weaver building to a design for his own needs; the new industrial housing, however, was a collective effort between speculative builder, landowner, mill owner, local government, and the new building societies, and the occupier himself played little part. Whereas the keynote of pre-industrial building was individuality in style, layout, and materials, that of the new factory era was uniformity. The long terraces of stone-built workers' cottages crowded on to the valley floors and when there was no more floor left grappled with the steep hillsides. As the old parishes swelled to bursting with their growing populations, new churches appeared in proportion to the growth of congregations, and uniformity in housing design was paralleled by the repetition of new Gothic style parish churches from end to end of the industrial north.

In these booming, bustling mill towns, the normal amenities of a civilised urban life such as street lighting, sewerage, piped water, public transport, and gas supply arrived only slowly and for a long time lagged behind the demands of the growing populations. Until 1828 Huddersfield was supplied with water only by a few small private companies, but in that year a new reservoir was built at Longwood. Even this, however, proved to be inadequate, and in 1844 use of water had to be restricted to certain days in the week. Gradually however as new strong local government took over the creaking machinery of parochial and Poor Law administration, the towns began to recognise the importance and to undertake the provision of public amenities. The erection of fine new public buildings including schools, libraries, town halls, public baths, market halls, and weavers' or mechanics' institutes reflected a new civic awareness and made up for the lack of architectural expression in housing. Some buildings were on a grandiose scale: Todmorden Magistrate's Court, formerly the Town Hall, is built in the Greek Parthenon style with a frontage of massive columns and a pediment carrying pseudo-classical figures holding an engine crankshaft, a box of spindles, and a bale of cotton, symbols of the town's prosperity (Fig 19). It was, however, in the architecture of the many Methodist chapels that the dignity of the new working classes found its chief expression. The

19 Todmorden Magistrates' Court. Public buildings often of classical proportions relieved the drab uniformity of housing in the growing industrial towns.

several schisms of the Methodist church were partly responsible for the proliferation of chapels, which far outnumber parish churches, their stark symmetrical frontages providing the focal points of the urban scene.

The impact of the new towns spread beyond the cobbled streets with their mills, houses, and chapels and on to the hills and moors beyond. The rapid population growth of the early nineteenth century increased the demand for food and for a time made profitable the cultivation of moorland slopes and plateaux which had been dismissed by earlier generations as unworthy of human effort. The consequence was a final phase of moorland reclamation and enclosure which in many districts carried the dry stone walling up to the moorland summits. Enclosure was most widespread where large tracts of unappropriated commons remained from earlier generations, but was absent where rich land-owners had secure ownership of grouse moors. Thus the moors between Blackburn and Bolton to the east of Darwen were broken up by the new fields, whereas those west of Darwen stretching towards Anglezarke remained private shooting grounds. The agricultural potential of the newly broken moorlands was greatly overestimated: the highly acid windswept soils could never hope to yield grain profitably once cheaper imported colonial cereals became widely available. Within a generation of enclosure many new fields had been abandoned and had reverted to rough pasture. The depressed agricultural conditions of the later nineteenth century began the desertion of farms built on the new enclosures, and the retreat of farming to more appropriate margins has continued into the present century.

Although the moorlands could not become the granaries of the growing towns, they nevertheless satisfied the great thirst generated by urban growth. Huddersfield's first moorland reservoir of 1828 was followed by eight more during the course of the century, giving the town a water capacity of 1,715 million gallons drawn from a catchment area of 51,824 acres. By the end of the century the higher valleys of the central Pennines had been transformed into great water gathering grounds for the neighbouring conurbations.

The industrialisation and urbanisation of the central Pennines achieved by the combined efforts of mill owner and landowner, weaver and labourer, owed much to the contribution of particular individuals and families. Some captains of industry carved highly individual marks on the face of the region by creating entire communities. Ramsbottom in lower Rossendale was largely a creation of the Grant brothers by whom it was controlled until the 1860s. In 1806 they bought the print works established there since 1783 and in 1821 built a cotton mill, and around these factories built streets of workers' cottages. In 1832 William Grant added a Presbyterian church and completed the new community by building on the hillside a folly commemorating the family. The folly was brought to the ground by a gale in 1943, but Ramsbottom itself remains the family's monument. Across the Pennines Colonel Edward Akroyd created mill communities at Copley and Boothtown near Halifax. Like Ramsbottom, they are reminders of the entrepreneurs who brought so much change to the Pennine scene in the last century.

By 1900 the landscape of today had largely taken shape. The region was at its most populous and the most formative elements in its personality had emerged. Concrete and tarmacadam have since added much that is new but little that is distinctive. Moreover the bulldozer has become an ever-growing threat to the region's cultural heritage. The following chapters will look at this heritage in more detail.

**Selected further reading:**

J. Aikin, *Description of the Country from Thirty to Forty Miles around Manchester*, 1795

E. Baines, *Account of the Woollen Manufacture of England (1858)*, ed K. G. Ponting, David & Charles, 1969

R. Brook, *The Story of Huddersfield*, Macgibbon & Kee, 1968

G. H. Tupling, *The Economic History of Rossendale*, Manchester, 1927

T. W. Woodhead, *History of the Huddersfield Water Supplies*, Tolson Memorial Museum, Huddersfield, 1939

# 5 Hamlets, Villages and Towns

Settlements are a principal feature of any man-made landscape, for they are not only man's dwelling places but are also the focal points around which social and economic activity revolves. Unlike some landscape features which remain largely unaltered through time, settlements are in a constant state of change. They grow and contract with population size, while at the same time their layouts change in response to the varying social and economic patterns of each generation of inhabitants. Each settlement may thus be a product of several decades or even of several centuries of growth. Recent developments and changes sometimes obliterate earlier forms, but in other instances rebuilding preserves the original plan, fossilising it within a modern fabric.

The central Pennines display a wide variety of settlement forms, a reflection of the long history of human occupation and changes in the economic pattern over the centuries. Settlements vary in scale from scattered farms and hamlets to villages, towns, and the outer edges of sprawling urban regions. Many settlements have changed their function several times in their history, starting life as agricultural hamlets, then becoming industrial villages, and finally finding a twentieth century role as dormitory settlements of the West Yorkshire or Manchester conurbations. Each is unique, but distinctive patterns and plans are nevertheless discernible.

## Pre-Norman villages

The earliest settlements, the villages of Bronze and Iron Age settlers, long ago vanished from the face of the region. The location of their dwellings is unknown and the only remains of their occupation are barrows (burial chambers) and relics of occasional hill forts. It is very difficult to show any continuity between these features and present day settlements, and they are mostly of interest to the archaeologist.

The oldest settlements occupied continuously since their origins are the villages of the Anglians who colonised the region from the late sixth century onwards. The majority of their villages were established in Airedale and through the Craven lowlands into mid-Ribblesdale, but others were founded along the northern boundary of the region down the Wenning and Lune valleys, and also in lower Calderdale. South of the Ribble and Aire these villages grew into industrial towns and their original village forms largely disappeared with the advent of mills and industrial housing, but northwards there are several well-preserved examples.

Clifton near Brighouse is a village in industrial West Yorkshire which has managed to preserve its character despite the surge of industry around it. Some aspects of its form have remained largely unaltered since Anglian times and it demonstrates characteristically Anglian features. Clifton stands on a ridge 200 ft above the plain of the river Calder, and until recently formed a 'street' settlement in which most of the dwellings faced each other across a single half-mile long main thoroughfare. Comparison of the modern map with a village plan of 1788 suggests however that this may not always have been the case. Dwellings on the northern side of the main street in 1788 were backed by a row of small plots or crofts. These can still be found today and represent the area intensively tilled by the first inhabitants. Beyond these crofts towards the boundaries of the township stretched the open fields representing the reclamations of subsequent medieval generations. Across the street from the long north row of houses was another, discontinuous row, backed not by crofts but by irregularly-shaped fields enclosed from the village's former common reaching down to the Calder. It seems probable that the north side of the street is the original Anglian settlement, the villagers pasturing their livestock on the open common fronting their dwellings. Gradually encroachments on this common led to the growth of a south row of houses and also of a back lane parallel to this south row. Post-war development has been gradually filling in the gaps along the south side of the main street.

Bowland and Craven have villages with similar characteristics to Clifton. Grindleton also developed along a single main street, in which one row of houses is backed by crofts which in turn back on to the former open fields. The street runs from south to north up the slope of the hill, and begs the question of why the original settlers preferred this alignment with its steep gradient to a much easier east to west orientation along the foot of the slope. The answer appears to lie in the economic pattern of the early community. In this hill country livestock rearing was more important than arable cultivation, and livestock movements between valley meadow and hill pasture were a regular part of village life. The upslope orientation of the road and dwellings was the

20 Downham in the Ribble valley is an Anglian village first recorded in the twelfth century. It stands on the slope of a ridge of high land overlooked by Pendle Hill.

most convenient layout which permitted these movements.

A neighbouring village, West Bradford, had a quite different plan. Today dwellings straggle along the main lane in both the Waddington and Grindleton directions and an irregular scatter of buildings stretches from this lane southwards towards the Ribble. Early maps show that this latter locality was originally an open green which was largely free from building in 1765 and only partly encroached upon by 1848. A cotton mill later occupied some of the remaining area. In medieval times the green provided an area where poor people could tether their livestock and where all stock could be driven for protection in case of attack. North of the village Eaves House marks the site of a breakaway settlement established by squatters in Tudor times on the 'eaves' or edge of the village; it never flourished and today only this building and some small farmhouses mark its position.

Slaidburn in the upper Hodder valley was a settlement of local importance in the medieval period. It was the administrative centre of the manor of Slaidburn which included most of the upper Hodder area, and its parish church dates back to the eleventh century. Surprisingly it was never granted a market charter although fairs were held regularly. Its buildings cluster around the meeting of four lanes above the flood level of the river and include the Grammar School (1717), corn mill and the inn which was once the seat of the manor courts. The inn was only the most recent of Slaidburn's court houses, for the manor court rolls record the building of an earlier court house in 1577 on land now occupied by the school. There appears to have been a great deal of new building in sixteenth-century Slaidburn, for the court rolls record building along waysides leading from the village centre, particularly Shay Lane (the west road) and the north road called the Skaithe, a district now without houses. A secondary settlement grew up at the far end of the townfield called the High Field, for a sixteenth-century map shows several dwellings grouped around an open green. Today only two farms mark the site of this abortive village, but the green around which the houses stood is clearly visible.

Slaidburn is an example of a village which flourished and grew in medieval times but others were not so fortunate and, for reasons which can only be speculated upon languished and decayed. The site of such 'deserted' villages is often only recoverable by careful documentary, map, and field research. This is the case with an old township in the same district called Easington, recorded in Domesday Book (1086) and with a population of thirteen households in 1379. The modern map marks an extensive parish called Easington to the north of Slaidburn, but it consists wholly of dispersed farms and contains no single settlement named Easington which could represent the medieval vill. Nineteenth-century maps however show that old Easington comprised not only the portion already described but also a smaller separated portion along the Hodder west of Slaidburn and now in Newton parish. Moreover this small portion contains a farmstead named Easington standing near a field named 'The Green' and close to other fields with names suggesting they once formed part of a common field system. The 'Green' is clearly seen today and nearby are mounds which might perhaps be the sites of old buildings. It is undoubtedly this Easington which is the village of 1086 and 1379, a group of buildings surrounding an open green and with a common open field. For some reason unrecorded the larger detached portion was added at a later date by which time the original settlement was in decay. Modern boundary changes have obscured, but not eradicated, the original settlement history.

## Forest hamlets

Away from Airedale and Ribblesdale and their tributary valleys there are few of the large compact villages just described. Instead the initial settlement took the form of dispersed farms and hamlets, many of which were not created until later medieval times. This is particularly the case in the formerly extensive forest lands. Here settlement was initiated by domainal cattle farms or vaccaries (Chapter 2) or by squatters. With the passage of time as further woodlands and heathlands were cleared, these homesteads grew into clusters of dwellings.

Many forest settlements developed into industrial villages at a later period, and so lost their early form, but some escaped the spread of industry and retain their original character. A good example is Wycoller near Colne, (Fig 21) originally one of three vaccaries of the Forest of Trawden. Wycoller lies along the sheltered Wycoller Beck and its grazing lands extended up the valley on to the moors as far as the main Pennine watershed on Combe Hill and Crow Hill. The name of Herders Hill recalls this period of Wycoller's history. By 1527 the

21 Wycoller, a weaving hamlet in the Forest of Trawden. Teams of packhorses crossed the stream by the bridge in the foreground. Field walling made of vertical stone blocks can be seen above the cottages.

vaccary had been divided into six holdings and the old homestead had become a hamlet. Between the Tudor period and the Industrial Revolution it became a handloom weaving centre of local importance and lay astride a packhorse route from Colne to Keighley. Today Wycoller is deserted but there is still much to remind the visitor of its former character. Wycoller Hall, described in Chapter 6, was a typical home of a Pennine squire and nearby can be found its cockfighting pit and fishpond. Ruined cottages have marks on the walls indicating former hand-loom weaving, and the two-arched bridge over the stream recalls the packhorse era. The hamlet and its vicinity are now a Conservation Area and Country Park.

The forest hamlets are most widely preserved however north of the Ribble amongst the moors of Bowland and Wyresdale. Whitewell is a picturesque settlement sited where the Hodder cuts a gorge through the lower Bowland hills, and is overlooked by wooded limestone knolls. It originated as a lodge for the keepers of the Forest of Bowland, and the forest court rolls record the holding of courts here at which forest dwellers were fined for felling timber and hunting deer. In 1570 this court heard about 'the killing of a hind in Ashurst Hey in the forest about Peter Day...by Nicholas Battersby and John Heyke, the same Heyke confessed the same to the Master Forester.' This court also fined various people for taking timbers, including one William Isherwood the saddler 'for felling a great alder, three small alders, and four hollins...likewise the same William for cropping of the saplings and felling of the yarding at inconvenient times of the year.' The site of the lodge is now occupied by an hotel and close to it stands the chapel of ease erected about 1400 for the inhabitants of this remote district and for travellers on the lonely road from Clitheroe to Lancaster.

The road leads northwards into the narrow pass or Trough of Bowland, at the entrance to which is the hamlet of Sykes, which like Wycoller originated as a forest vaccary. Sykes developed where a headstream of the Hodder cuts through a basin of shale and limestone, providing more sheltered and fertile land than the surrounding gritstone moors. In 1527 there were nine small farms at Sykes including an outlying farmstead at Trough House, and each holding comprised some small scattered walled fields in the limestone basin. All the farmers shared the common rough grazing of the four thousand acres of surrounding moorland. By 1845 consolidation had reduced the number of holdings to five, and since then all the holdings have been combined into one large sheep farm. The hamlet today consists of this farm and an adjoining row of cottages.

Another old Bowland settlement called Beatrix reveals much about the development and structure of forest hamlets. Beatrix was created by the Norsemen (Chapter 2) but during the later Middle Ages became a forest vaccary. By the seventeenth century it had been broken up into eleven tenant holdings, largely as a result of subdivision of the property within the tenant families. In the north of England it was for long the custom for a father not to leave all his land to his eldest son but to divide it between several sons, and this practice contributed markedly to the creation of new holdings, particularly in old forest areas such as Bowland. As a result of this subdivision, in 1765 there were nine occupiers of land at Beatrix with holdings varying in size from 14 to 154 acres. Three holdings lay on the edge of the old vaccary land, and one of these has since grown into the modern hamlet of Dunsop Bridge. The dwellings of the remaining six holdings were clustered on the original site and their

22 Beatrix in 1765. Holdings A and B formed part of the main hamlet and their parcels of land were dispersed. Holding C, the outlying farm at Wood End, had a consolidated portion of land. The northern half of Beatrix was unenclosed moorland grazing.

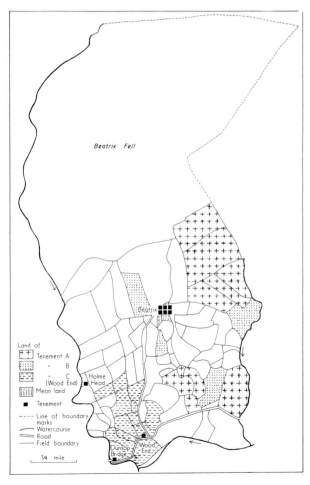

lands were very fragmented (Fig 22). All farmers had the use of the unenclosed Beatrix Fell. Today there is again only one farm at Beatrix, and its former hamlet structure has disappeared. Many of the hedges present in 1765 have since been uprooted and others realigned so that only fragments now survive of the Tudor field pattern.

The best preserved of Bowland's forest hamlets is Harrop Fold, located on the eastern side of the old forest where an ancient earthwork called the Harrop or Champion Dyke marked the forest's eastern march. Part of this boundary is still traceable parallel to the Grindleton to Slaidburn road. Harrop Fold itself shelters beneath the steep slopes of Harrop Fell and comprises two farms and three cottages half a mile from the public road. The lane to the hamlet passes a house converted into a chapel to minister to this tiny isolated community. The settlement's very remoteness perhaps provides the key to the survival of such forest hamlets through the profound industrial and social changes of the nineteenth and twentieth centuries.

## Industrial villages

Industrial villages are the most common settlement form in the central Pennines. South of the Ribble and Aire there are few valleys whch do not possess one or more, usually grouped round a mill or bleachworks. Along some valleys industrial villages have merged to form a continuous built-up area, as in Rossendale where old settlements at Constable Lee, Crawshaw Booth, Goodshaw, Love Clough, and Dunnockshaw have joined to produce a long string of houses and mills along the Limy Water north of Rawtenstall. In some places industrial settlements grew up next to older ones. The Rossendale hamlet of Goodshaw stands on high ground astride a packhorse road and adjoins a sixteenth-century chapel of ease; half a mile away down in the valley is Goodshaw Fold with workers' houses close to nineteenth-century water-powered mills.

Where mill villages grew around older settlements they show clear evidence of continuity between the domestic and factory textile eras. This is the case with villages along the southern flanks of Pendle Hill such as Barrowford, already a populous settlement in the middle of the seventeenth century. By 1800 hand-loom weaving was well established, and Barrowford grew rapidly in the early nineteenth century from 1,224 persons in 1801 to 2,633 in 1831. The trade benefited by the opening of the Marsden, Gisburn, and Long Preston turnpike through the village in 1803, and there are several rows of hand-loom weavers' cottages dating from the early nineteenth century. The new road ran close to Barrowford Brook, and the double advantage of water and transport was

23  Wheatley Lane, Pendle, a medieval hamlet which grew into a mill village.
Early nineteenth-century housing, including a three-storey weaver's cottage, is on
the right; later nineteenth-century houses line the left side of the road.

favourable to the building of cotton mills. By 1844 the village stretched
continuously along the turnpike from the church at Lowerford to the
farther side of Higherford. Thereafter the impetus of mill development
passed to less congested sites along the canal and railway at Nelson two
miles away. Today Barrowford is an outlying district of the Burnley
mini-conurbation, to which it is joined by unbroken urban development
along the road to Nelson.

In other villages the continuity between industrial growth and earlier
development is less apparent. Denholme on the moors between Halifax
and Keighley was in the eighteenth century a walled park, and Jefferys'
map of 1772 shows the park boundary with gates at the northern
(Cullingworth Gate) and southern (Denholme Gate) ends, but there
were few buildings and no signs of the present village. By 1847 however
there were two distinct clusters of dwellings, a mining community
along the main road near coal pits and including the Methodist chapel,
and another housing area called the New Road Side almost half a mile
down the road at the bottom of the hill beside a worsted mill on the

Carporley Beck. The great mills which now dominate the landscape were not built until 1851, and thereafter the area between the two settlements was filled in by terraces of houses and short streets off the road. Another Yorkshire village, Meltham Mills, south of Huddersfield, was more clearly a creation entirely of the Industrial Revolution. It lies on a headwater of Mag Brook, and until 1780 the site was merely a wild moorland clough with the pre-Conquest village of Meltham on one side and the hamlet of Thick Hollins on the other. In 1780 William Brook built a scribbling mill and Nathaniel Dyson added a fulling mill in 1786. Brook then built a woollen mill and in the early nineteenth century his son Jonas changed from wool to cotton manufacture. The village grew around these mills and thus has wholly different origins from the older village of Meltham on the hillside above.

The Lancashire village of Belmont is likewise a product of the factory age. Until 1801 its site was a windswept ridge of moorland in the ancient township of Sharples. In that year the moor was crossed by the Sharples to Hoghton turnpike, the last link in the new road from Bolton to Preston, and in 1804 the 'bottom' printworks, later used as a bleachworks and dyeworks, was opened close to where the road crosses Hordern Brook. Maria Square, a terraced row of cottages off the new road and immediately above the works was built and named after the daughter of the Ryecroft family which founded the works. Later the 'top' works, a cotton mill subsequently converted to a bleachworks, was built higher up the valley. Both works obtained water from the Hordern Brook until the construction of the Belmont Reservoir for Bolton in 1826 provided an alternative supply. The village grew rapidly and its population exceeded 1,000 by 1845. New terraces appeared along and off the High Street, including on the east side of the High Street three-storey houses each occupied by two families. The parish church of St Peter was consecrated in 1849. Belmont has seen little modern development; surrounded by moors on three sides, it straggles along the A675 for half a mile with no discernible focus, its strong linear form reflecting the importance of the road in the formative period of its development.

## Industrial colonies

A characteristic feature of regions affected by the Industrial Revolution was the growth of planned industrial communities. Amidst the general scramble for factory sites most industrialists were content to satisfy their workers' need for housing by the haphazard construction of terraces of utilitarian cottages on such odd scraps of land as were convenient. Some more thoughtful entrepreneurs however considered

24 Newtown, a hand-loom weaving settlement of the early nineteenth century. Top: layout of the cottages. Bottom: typical ground floor design of cottage with room for weaving or nailing.

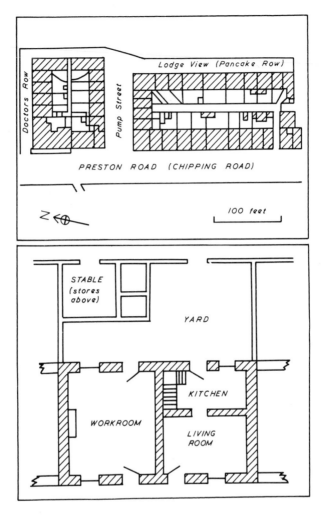

the desirability of providing workers not merely with housing but with a form of building development which would provide social, recreational, and spiritual amenities laid out in an orderly and aesthetically pleasing manner. This was the basis of the planned industrial colony. Some colonies hardly went beyond neat blocks of terraces with a doctor, chapel, or blacksmith but others were self-contained model villages.

Although principally associated with the factory age, the idea pre-dates the coming of factories and was a feature of the late domestic industry period. At Longridge, an outlying mill town on the western Pennine flanks, there is a small locality called Newtown which consists of two rectangular blocks of terraced houses (Fig 24). They were built between 1825 and about 1840 by one Dr Edmund Eccles whose own easily distinguishable larger house formed part of the community. Some thirty houses were built, the two blocks being separated by a broad street (Pump Street). Each house had a through workroom at the side of the living quarters, and most of the occupants were domestic weavers although there were two nailers who also repaired looms. One household specialised in dressing, combing, and straightening the warps, and another building was used as a warehouse for storing the completed material. The community had a population of 207 in 1871.

Particularly striking among the planned communities of the factory age are the model villages of the Akroyds at Halifax. The Akroyds were already a long-established woollen manufacturing family in Halifax when in 1847 Colonel Edward Akroyd built a mill at Copley. Behind the mill he laid out an estate of terraced cottages in Gothic style with mullioned and transomed windows and arched doorways, (Fig 25). He also provided a school, library, and canteen for his workmen. Across the bridge in 1863 he built the striking church of St Stephen. The mill is now demolished, but the village survives unaltered. Akroyd repeated his experiment a few years later at his Haley Hill mills at Boothtown on the other side of Halifax. As at Copley the housing was built in Gothic fashion, the streets being named after cathedral cities. Overlooking the community he built his own mansion, now the Bankfield Museum.

25　Copley, a factory village built by the mill-owning Akroyd family of Halifax.

The largest and most well known example of a Pennine factory community is Saltaire on the edge of the Bradford conurbation near Shipley. Baines in 1858 described Sir Titus Salt's community as 'probably unequalled in the world for extent and completeness, and it is still rapidly growing'. The mill and its ancillary buildings cover almost ten acres. On a further twenty-five acres Salt built 820 homes between 1850 and 1872, providing accommodation for over 4,400 people. The houses were built in rectangular blocks of sixteen to a row, with a parlour, kitchen, two or three bedrooms, and yard but no garden. He also built a school, a Congregational Church, and an Institute which according to Baines 'in respect of the amplitude and excellence of the resources it offers for the study and recreation of receivers of weekly wages, is unrivalled in the kingdom'. On the other side of the Aire he provided a fourteen-acre park leading up on to the hillside beyond. The estate, once in open country, now stands absorbed by the northward spread of the Bradford conurbation on to the moors between the Aire and the Wharfe.

## Market towns and industrial towns

The first Pennine towns were market centres at which local farmers sold and exchanged their produce. The right to hold markets was originally a jealously guarded privilege obtainable only by royal charter, but eventually some places succeeded in acquiring market rights by showing that markets had been regularly held in the past.

By the seventeenth century there were several Pennine market centres. Some, such as West Bradford near Clitheroe, never grew beyond villages; but others, such as Rochdale and Halifax had by the Industrial Revolution attained considerable status beyond their immediate locality. They represent the beginnings of Pennine urban life.

Many of these towns grew into industrial centres long ago, submerging their original market function, but one which escaped the tide of industrialism, preserving its market character, was Skipton. It originated as an Anglian sheep farm which by Norman times had grown into a sizeable village flanked by two townfields. The spur to Skipton's growth was the building of the castle by the Norman baron Romille as the centre of the new Honour of Skipton, and by the twelfth century a market to serve the needs of the castle was being held around a market cross in what is now the High Street. During the Middle Ages this street, which partly subdivides to form Sheep Street, became the focal point of the growing settlement with houses down either side backed by long gardens extending on the west side as far as Ellerbeck. At the northern end below the castle the High Street divided to form the roads to Lancaster and York; at the southern end it gave access to the roads to Otley and Clitheroe. During Stuart times many houses were rebuilt in stone, and further refacing took place in the eighteenth century. By this time Skipton was well established as the principal wool, beef, and corn market of Craven. Newmarket Street marks the site of its extended corn mart. By 1800 Skipton was also becoming a centre of the worsted trade, and the use for coal transport of the Leeds and Liverpool Canal, which reached the town in 1774, gave impetus to its growth as an industrial centre. This new chapter of Skipton's history resulted in a quintupling of population during the nineteenth century. Industrialisation however kept away from the old town centre and throughout the scramble for commercial sites the layout of the medieval centre remained largely intact.

The same however is not true for Burnley, the medieval market character of which was wholly transformed by industrial growth. Medieval Burnley was a hamlet clustered around the parish church in the district later called Top o'the Town; here there was a market cross, stocks, a fulling mill, and various houses and tradesmens' premises fronting an old trackway following a terrace of the river Brun down to the Calder bridge. This thoroughfare was to become Burnley's main street. By 1650 this road linked the original settlement with another hamlet called Bridge End, later known as Westgate, clustered around the bridge. By 1800 the growth of the handloom weaving trade was bringing about the expansion of this nucleus and its coalescence with neighbouring hamlets.

Burnley's historian Walter Bennett distinguishes two phases in the town's growth during the nineteenth century. Between 1800 and 1850 the rudimentary but comfortable farm cottage building tradition of the previous century gave way to crowded and airless back-to-back houses, cellar dwellings, and tenement houses. Such dwellings had no domestic drainage or water supply so that waste water had to be emptied directly into the streets, while the unpaved alleys and court which riddled the buildings were frequently choked with garbage. The worst houses were the cellar dwellings, devoid of light and fresh air and often with ceilings below the level of the roadway. In 1867 there were 298 cellar dwellings occupied by nearly a thousand persons, and families of between six and ten persons per dwelling were commonplace. Yards and courts were frequently used for hen-cotes, pig-sties, and cowsheds, and the danger to public health from overcrowding and lack of essential amenities was enormous. The houses jostled for space with each other and with the older houses, inns, shops, stables, workshops, and warehouses so that 'inn yards were filled with the workshops of tradesmen, houses were built on to the backs of mills, and hovels were clustered behind the buildings on the main street'. The result was an irregular, chaotic street plan which stifled movement and prohibited improvements.

After 1850 the expansion of Burnley was rapid. Its 5,000 houses of 1851 had increased to 12,000 by 1871 and to 21,000 by 1901. Much new building took place in the growing industrial areas of Fulledge and Accrington Road, and its character was quite different from that of the earlier phase. The Third Burnley Improvement Act of 1854 appointed Improvement Commissioners with powers to control building development, while new regulations ensured a higher standard of building construction. Thenceforth each house was to have its own yard, water closet, and sewerage, and rooms were to be of a minimum height. From this time until the early years of the present century date the highly regular street layouts of much of the town, and many of these houses, can still be found despite post-war demolition. These artisans' dwellings commonly had four or five rooms, the better ones six rooms, a lobby, and small front garden. At the same time a thorough remodelling of the town centre was undertaken, involving the widening and realignment of St James' Street and other main thoroughfares, together with the eradication of the many 'beggarly huts and wretched shops' in the way of the scheme. By this means much of the worst property built early in the century was removed. Town centre public buildings appeared, including a market hall, town hall, grammar school, workhouse, and theatre. Street lighting was introduced on main streets although not on back streets until 1913. Parks and recreation grounds were created, sometimes from private donations of land, the most important example being the sale to the Corporation in 1896 of Towneley Hall and its 61-acre grounds by Lady O'Hagan for a fraction of its real value.

Unlike Burnley some smaller Pennine towns had no medieval origins and began as amalgamations of several expanding industrial hamlets, attaining municipal autonomy during the nineteenth century. Oswaldtwistle near Accrington is an example. Although a vill of Oswaldtwistle was recorded in 1311, there is no evidence to suggest that this formed the nucleus of the modern settlement. The Oswaldtwistle of today grew up alongside the present Union Road, until 1827 the principal route from Blackburn to Accrington. By 1780 there were a number of hamlets along this route between Stanhill and Church, and thereafter factory growth provided the basis for industrial housing developments. One of the earliest factories was the Foxhill Bank Printworks (1780) which had associated housing at Duncan Square, Badge Brow, and adjoining parts of Union Road. Nearby in the same road the extensive Moscow Mill complex (1824-28) had workers' housing at George, Queen and Frederick Streets. Still further along Union Road are the Stonebridge

Mills (1845) and Rhyddings Mill (1856), again flanked by streets of terraced workers' housing. At the northern end of the town the Hoghton family built Rhoden and Roegreave Mills (1860-2), and the Roegreave Road housing area, and were instrumental in founding Holy Trinity Church. By the end of the century these various mill communities had merged to form a continuous built-up area. The Stanhill Ring Spinning Mill (1906) gave rise to the West End housing area a mile from the main part of the town. This piecemeal growth has meant that Oswaldtwistle has no distinct town centre, its Town Hall being but one of various public buildings, churches, shops, mills, and houses which stretch from the Church boundary for over a mile towards New Lane. Union Road provides the town's only unifying thread. In 1974 Oswaldtwistle lost its municipal independence and became part of the larger Borough of Hyndburn centred on Accrington. The absence of new commercial development is a symptom of the town's economic decline, and its future seems to lie more and more as an outlying district of its larger neighbour.

Perhaps Huddersfield is the epitome of the Pennine industrial town. In 1780 it was merely a 'poor straggling town' on the banks of the Colne, comprising a huddle of buildings around its Cloth Hall and parish church. From these beginnings its many mills spread along the valley floor towards Milnsbridge while housing areas climbed up the valley sides to absorb old hamlets at Crosland, Lindley, Almondbury, Fartown, and Lockwood. Friedrich Engels described Huddersfield in 1844 as 'the handsomest by far of all the factory towns of Yorkshire and Lancashire by reason of... its modern architecture', while today Pevsner finds the situation of the town, 'spectacular, the view of the smoking mills from the hills, or of the hills from the bottom of the valley, impressive if bleak'. Like many Pennine towns, it demonstrates the closeness of the relationship between physical landscape and human settlement.

**Selected further reading:**
W. Bennett, *The History of Burnley*, 4 vols Burnley, 1947-51
J. Bentley, *Portrait of Wycoller*, Nelson, 1975
R. Brook, *The Story of Huddersfield*, Macgibbon & Kee, 1968
D. Hogg, *A History of Church & Oswaldtwistle*, 2 vols Accrington, 1973
B. Roberts, *Rural Settlement in Britain*, Dawson, 1977
G.H. Tupling, 'The Origins of Markets and Fairs in Medieval Lancashire', *Transactions of the Lancashire & Cheshire Antiquarian Society*, vol 49 (1933)

# 6 Houses and Cottages

Domestic buildings form a principal element of any cultural landscape. Their features reveal a great deal about their builders and occupiers, their level of wealth, the materials they had available, and the economic, social and cultural characteristics of the period of building. In the central Pennines a wide variety of housing types can be seen. Not only was there a gradual change in building styles over the centuries, but the architecture of the region displays a close relationship between housing type and the social status of the inhabitants. Moreover, in previous centuries houses were often places of work, and their designs show the influence of domestic industries.

Until the seventeenth century only a minority of Pennine people, the gentry and a few wealthier townspeople, lived in buildings which by present-day standards we might consider substantial or comfortable. The rest of the population lived in primitive one-roomed houses of wood, clay, and thatch. The roofs were supported at either end by pairs of huge curving timbers called crucks which were tied where they met at the apex. There would be a primitive hearth in the middle of the floor and a hole in the roof immediately above to let out the smoke. Such 'firehouses' were the normal form of accommodation for the labouring poor and continued to be built well into the seventeenth century.

By 1630 a new phase of house building had become evident. Wealthy clothiers found the money to build themselves new stone houses, and the gradual downward percolation through society of this new wealth from the cloth industry enabled people of all social classes to rebuild their primitive houses in stone to more substantial and comfortable designs. From 1630 to 1850 Pennine domestic architecture attained qualities often termed vernacular, meaning closely influenced by the region's distinctive material resources, local styles, and the social and economic needs of the inhabitants. After 1850 the development of the railway enabled the rapid spread of all types of building materials so that from this time onwards Pennine building began to lose its distinctive features.

The local stone has contributed considerably to the development of a distinctive architectural tradition. The sandstones of the Millstone Grit and Coal Measures provide a durable building material, yellow when first quarried and gradually weathering to grey or black according to the amount of soot in the atmosphere. Until the middle of the last century this material was extensively used not only for walling and roofing but also for windows, doorways, and fireplaces. It was the skill of the mason in fashioning these latter features that was responsible for much of the interesting detail of Pennine houses.

## Large houses

There are few really large houses in the central Pennines, certainly none to equal in scale such stately homes as Chatsworth or Blenheim. This is because the land was too poor to support great lords who could afford to build grandiose palaces, but the region has several houses which are large compared to the majority of dwellings, and these were the houses of the landowning elite of society. They are of considerable architectural interest since each exhibits several phases of building and rebuiding. They are also the least 'vernacular' of Pennine houses; the wealth and social status of their occupiers ensured that these houses were influenced as much by national dictates in fashion as by local building traditions.

Perhaps the oldest of these large houses is Towneley Hall, Burnley, for seven centuries the residence of the Towneley family and now kept as an art gallery and museum by the Borough of Burnley. Towneley originated in the fourteenth century as a two-storey fortified house or pele tower, and the six-feet thick walls of the original dwelling still remain in the south-east wing. The rest of the house was added in the fifteenth century but subsequent modifications made Towneley largely post-medieval in structure. These include the short arched mullioned Jacobean upper windows overlooking the taller elegant Georgian windows of the lower floor. Mock castellating and turreting were added by Jeffrey Wyatt in 1817 to restore a medieval military character to the house. By this time the simple austere defensive tower of the late middle ages had been wholly absorbed by the developing structure. The pele tower was common in the restless north of England in the later medieval period and the central Pennines has other examples, one of which is Turton Tower near Bolton. Here the pele tower is still evident, although altered by the addition of Tudor half-timbered ranges as well as mullioned and transomed windows.

A second type of basic structure forming a starting point for the development of large houses was the half-timbered hall, originally a single room open to the roof to which later wings and passages were added. This was the origin of Shibden Hall, Halifax, built in the early fifteenth century by William Otes, a sheep farmer of Southowram, and in later centuries owned by the wealthy Lister family. At Shibden the old hall now forms the centre range, and originally consisted of a timber frame resting on a stone base, the spaces between the timbers being infilled with timber and plaster studding. Two cross gables were added later, and in the seventeenth century a new stone front replaced the original. Further substantial alterations were made in the 1830s by Anne Lister, so that today the internal and external structure of the house reflects her work and tastes rather than a gradual evolution over the centuries.

Shibden Hall represents a combination of the medieval timber and later stone building traditions. This combination is seen even more strikingly at Hall i' th' Wood, Bolton (Fig 26), known principally for its association with Samuel Crompton, inventor of the Spinning Mule. Like Shibden, this originated as a timber framed hall about 1500. The original portion of the building has some fine examples of timber panelling. Stone ranges were added on the north side in 1591 and on the south-west in 1648. The 1648 section includes deeply mullioned transomed windows, conical baluster pinnacles, and a double porch with arched

26   Hall i' th' Wood, Bolton. This house was built by the Brownlow family about 1500 and has remained largely unaltered since the mid-seventeenth century. It was presented to Bolton Corporation in 1900 and is now a museum of pre-industrial life.

doorway and decorative sundial. These features are all highly characteristic of the period and are also found on the 'Halifax' houses being built at the same period on the other side of the Pennines. The house has remained unaltered since then although it underwent restoration at the beginning of the century and reflects the contrasting building styles of the two centuries.

The break-up of old forests in the sixteenth century provided the opportunity for the emergence of a new landowning class, some of whom were able to build themselves substantial houses entirely of stone. An example is the Cunliffe family of Wycoller, near Colne, which acquired most of the land of the old forest vaccary of Wycoller and built Wycoller Hall about 1550. It had a central hall giving access at one end to a three-storey wing. At the other end of the hall was the main entrance via a double-storey porch, the door being surmounted by a jettied porch chamber window carrying heraldic emblems. The house is now in ruins, but one of the main features still intact is the massive hall fireplace 9 ft high and 16 ft wide with a stone bench behind the hearth to allow guests to sit round the fire (Fig 27). A nearby stone-framed doorway leading to the kitchen is dated 1596. Outdoors close by is a spacious aisled coach

27   The great fireplace at Wycoller Hall. The fire was made up in the centre, guests sitting on the ledge around it. The keyhole-shaped alcove was a wig-powdering cupboard.

house with high arched doorways now walled up.

Another house created out of old forest land in the sixteenth century is Browsholme, near Whitewell, built about 1603 by the Parker family, long-standing tenants of Bowland Forest. It has a 68 ft long central hall three storeys high flanked by two short wings. In 1805 Thomas Lister Parker added a new south-facing Georgian frontage in red sandstone with tall hooded sash windows and an arched doorway flanked by columns extending to the roof incorporating the three Greek orders. Landscaping of the gardens was also undertaken at this time, and a new entrance lodge built on the Whalley road with a front incorporating Elizabethan scrolls and a datestone for 1682. The house and estate are representative of the seat of a north country gentleman and of a social order now long passed away.

## 'Halifax' houses

The houses so far described were originally the dwellings of great landowning families. By Tudor and Stuart times however the growth of the cloth industry was leading to the emergence of a new social class with its own distinctive type of architecture. These merchant clothiers built themselves fine houses of spacious proportions reflecting their new wealth. Since so much of the cloth trade was focused on Halifax their houses are particularly prolific in that area, but they are by no means confined to it and examples can be found northwards into Ribblesdale, westwards into Lancashire, and as far east as Leeds.

The 'Halifax' houses date from between 1580 and 1680. Built entirely from stone, they provide most of the early examples of the new post-medieval stone building phase. They follow no single plan but demonstrate various layouts including H, E, square courtyard, and parallel gable plans. They nevertheless possess sufficient common features to be regarded as a distinctive regional architectural type. They are built of blocks of dressed stone, large blocks on the Millstone Grit areas, smaller blocks from the sandstones of the coalfield further east. Gables are mostly of low pitch and the roof ridges carry bold high stone chimneys. Windows are long and low, occupying much of the width of the room, and divided by vertical stone mullions into separate lights, often six or more. One window, usually the hall window, is taller and both mullioned and transomed, dividing it into as many as twelve lights. Stone drip-moulds above the windows keep off the rain (Fig 28). Particularly characteristic are the circular wheel or rose windows which illuminate the chambers above the doorways in the double-storey porches of several houses. Other external detail includes stone finials, ornamental

28  East Riddlesden Hall, Keighley, was built by James Murgatroyd, a wealthy clothier. It is now a museum in the hands of the National Trust.

drip-mould terminations, Tudor or ogee section doorway arches flanked by classical columns, and decorative doorway lintels with carved datestones.

A number of these old houses remain in the Ovenden valley, Halifax, once a quiet wooded vale extending almost as far as the old town centre but now becoming covered with urban sprawl. Grindlestone Bank, half-way up the valley, is a now much neglected old house with several gables and a double-storey porch. The house bears the dates 1603, 1647 and 1698, and the rear is joined by an arch carved with the name of the house to an outbuilding probably originally for wool storage. A little further down the valley is Spring Gardens or Lee House, with a similar porch to that at Grindlestone Bank, containing a plain Tudor door arch surmounted by a pair of mullioned windows in the porch chamber. Some eighteenth-century windows, including the tall, transomed staircase windows, provide evidence of later alteration. A short walk further on is Long Can, now divided into cottages. This house has a doorway lintel dated 1637 and carved with the initials of its occupiers, John and Mary

Murgatroyd. The windows are especially notable for their highly decorative and varied drip-mould terminations representing the acme of the development of this form of ornamentation.

South of the Calder there are other examples, some very fine. Barkisland Hall (1638) is a striking three-storey F-plan structure with large mullioned transomed windows across the frontage. The massive projecting porch has Doric columns flanking the entrance and Ionic columns alongside the transomed window of the first floor chamber. The upper storey porch chamber has a rose window with seven circular lights. Wood Lane Hall, Sowerby (1649) has a central hall flanked by two wings. The hall window is nine lights in width arranged in three groups of three further divided by two transoms, and the rose window above the porch is divided by curvilinear radial arms.

A prolific builder of Halifax houses was James Murgatroyd, a wealthy clothier, who after erecting several houses in the Halifax area for others, bought East Riddlesden Hall, Keighley, in 1638. Here along-

29 Some window and doorway features of houses in the Halifax area: **a** to **d** window drip-mould styles of houses along the Ovenden valley; **e** inscription over the doorway of Long Can, Ovenden: John and Mary Murgatroyd, 1637; **f** datestone of New House, Heptonstall, showing figures in early Georgian dress with the initials of Henry and Elizabeth Foster.

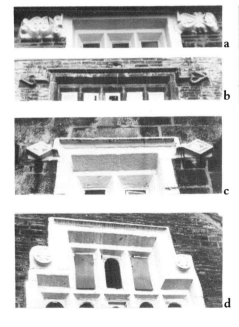

side the old dwelling he erected a handsome new house in the Halifax style (Fig 29). It has double-storey porches, one on either side of the house and each with an eight-spoke rose window with delicate tracery surmounted by mock battlements and finials. A plinth decorated with a scroll pattern runs round the south wing and the main doorway has Corinthian capitals. At East Riddlesden, as with other houses which have classical features, the strictly vernacular characteristics of the architecture were modified by the influence of contemporary fashion.


## Farmhouses and townhouses

The Pennines have few examples of farmhouses and townhouses surviving from before the seventeenth century. At Broad Bottom, Mytholmroyd, a fragment survives of medieval timber framing with wattle infill, and at Almondbury, Huddersfield, the now Conservative Association building is a partly timbered structure dated 1631, late for timber building. But on the whole the oldest surviving houses of farmers and more affluent townspeople are the all-stone buildings dating from after 1630 when stone building became general among this class of society.

Christopher Stell has produced a typology of Pennine farmhouses of the seventeenth and early eighteenth centuries based upon variations in internal plan. The feature common to these variations is the continued inclusion as a main room of the central hall which formed an important element in some of the large medieval houses already described. To this hall the builders added wings in various positions incorporating other rooms, access to which was frequently obtained from the hall by a cross-passage. Some houses had wings projecting towards the front at one or both ends, others had wings parallel to the hall at the rear while in yet other cases additional gables were omitted altogether and the rooms were incorporated under one long range. Externally these houses have many of the features of the clothiers' houses: walls of dressed stone-work, windows comprising long ranges of mullioned lights surmounted by drip-moulds, and ornamental doorways and lintels.

Such houses are very common throughout the region and particularly good examples are to be found on the moors around Hebden Bridge. Hippins, near Blackshaw Head, dated 1650, is one of these. In plan it has a central hall with a parlour at one end and a cross-passage at the other running behind the chimney stack giving access to the front door and further rooms. Externally it has a long, low appearance, and its features include straight chamfered mullioned windows, drip-moulds with decorative terminals, a Tudor lintel over the door, and stone pinnacles at the junctions of the eaves and gables

By the middle of the eighteenth century important changes were taking place in Pennine architectural styles. The varied plan types described above were giving way to a more regular design based on classical principles. There was a strong tendency to seek frontal symmetry by central positioning of the front door making it the focal point

30  Pennine windows. Window styles in Pennine houses reflect both changing social conditions and considerations of fashion. Early seventeenth-century windows had chamfered-section mullions dividing up the window into a long series of lights, were sometimes transomed, ie further divided by a horizontal member, and surmounted by a drip-mould with ornamental terminations (1a). Some seventeenth-century windows had semi-circular headed lights derived from medieval church window styles (1b). As the century progressed the drip-mould lost its ornamental terminations (1b) and by the eighteenth century had itself disappeared (1c).

By 1750 square section mullions had replaced the earlier chamfered style (2a) and long ranges of these types of lights are often found in weavers' cottages. Sometimes the centre light of a range was made slightly higher than the rest (2b) or given a semicircular head (2c). After 1800 mullions became thicker and fewer, windows were divided by wooden framing into smaller lights (2d and 2e), and sometimes sliding sashes were fitted. Georgian houses with higher rooms had taller windows but there was a reluctance to abandon mullions (2f).

With the spread of industrial housing in the nineteenth century the vertically sliding sash window became very common. At first these had small panes (3a) but fewer larger panes gradually became more common and after 1875 windows became taller and deeper to comply with improved housing stand-

ards (3b). The mullioned tradition nevertheless persisted in stone divisions between double windows (3c).

There were many variations on the above styles. Moreover innovations in design were adopted first in houses of the higher classes of society, only later spreading to the dwellings of labouring men, and the old styles continued in use for outbuildings such as barns long after their obsolescence for dwelling quarters. Changes were adopted first on frontages and on ground floors, only later on upper floors, in workrooms such as loomshops, and at the rear of buildings.

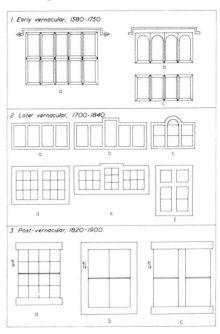

1. Early vernacular, 1580-1750

2. Later vernacular, 1700-1840

3. Post-vernacular, 1820-1900

of the frontage. The door was now flanked by a large window on each side surmounted by matching upper floor windows. The long layouts of the previous century gave way to shorter houses two rooms deep, with a staircase at the opposite end of the vestibule from the front door and lit by a tall staircase window. As rooms became higher windows changed in shape to let in more light; the long mullioned window gave way through a varied transition to the tall wooden framed sash window, the stone mullions being remarkably slow to disappear even though they gradually became fewer, broader, and simpler in section (Fig 30). These 'Georgian' houses arrived late in the Pennines (about 1730) but persisted until the later nineteenth century: they were erected sometimes as farmhouses but more particularly as the homes of better-off villagers and townspeople.

Longfield House, Heptonstall, is an early example of a Georgian style town house built around 1730. It has a symmetrical plan with a pedimented doorway and tall windows which nevertheless retain thick stone mullions and transoms. At Barrowford, Pendle, a seventeenth century house called Crowtrees was rebuilt in 1805 with a central front entrance incorporating a semi-circular stone arch and keystone surmounting a fanlight with radial tracery. Syke House in the same village, also dating from the early nineteenth century, has a long tall rear staircase window terminating at the top in a semi-circular arch with intersecting tracery. In Barrowford the Georgian style persisted well into the century, Thorneyclough being built to this design as late as 1871.

One very distinctive farmhouse type is the laithe house, in which both the dwelling and laithe (ie barn and mistal) are accommodated under a single roof. Laithe house construction spanned the entire vernacular building era and was particularly common on the new enclosures of the early nineteenth century. Laithe houses were invariably the homes of poorer farmers to whom some economy in construction was afforded by a reduction in the number of walls and whose small holdings required no large amount of space for cattle and hay storage. Human and animal accommodation are quite separate although there may be a communicating door between the two portions of the building.

Harkers, Slaidburn, is a good example of the type. Its window style suggests a date of about 1840 although the roughly cut stonework may represent an earlier structure. The living accommodation, taking up about a third of the building, consists of one room behind the other on each floor. The central barn area is approached through an arch wide enough to take a hay cart and the other end of the building is the mistal with space for one or two horses and about six cows. In 1844 Harkers was a farm of 50 acres of poor quality pasture, a size fairly typical of laithe house holdings.

# Weavers' cottages

Old weavers' cottages are widespread in the central Pennines. Cloth manufacture was a common occupation in the region long before the Industrial Revolution and most farmhouses had a room set aside for this activity where the farmer and his household would work at spinning wheels and a hand loom at times when little work could be done outdoors. The kitchen was often taken over for this purpose, a new kitchen being built at the rear of the house. As the eighteenth century progressed however a growing number of households became exclusively concerned with cloth making, and especially with weaving once the mechanisation of spinning and carding made yarn available in much greater quantities. By the 1780s cottages were being built specifically for the purpose of housing weavers working at home, and such houses continued to be built until the hand weaving trade declined. Few houses were built after 1840 other than in places where, for special reasons, hand-loom weaving persisted late. Hand weaving disappeared first in the cotton districts, somewhat later in the woollen areas. Middleton Rochdale, specialised in silk weaving, and here, because of the delicate nature of the work requiring considerable manual skills, hand loom weavers' cottages were erected into the 1860s.

The principal requirement for a weaver's cottage was a well lighted room separate from the living accommodation and some space to store yarn and finished cloth. In some cases this could be achieved without specialised architecture and so many former weavers' cottages are externally indistinguishable from other houses. On the other hand the trade gave rise to distinctive architectural features, and it is houses exhibiting these which are of special interest. In the hillside villages around Huddersfield such as Golcar and spreading across the main Pennine watershed into the Saddleworth and Littleborough districts many cottages can be found of two or three storeys with noticeably more window lights in the upper floors than in the ground floor. These upper windows, consisting of several long lights running almost the length of the cottages and separated by thick square-section mullions, illuminate the workrooms where two or three looms would once have been housed. Such houses, commonly built along the steep hillsides, have their first floor rear sides at ground level, and here a blocked in doorway can often be seen. To avoid carrying material through the dwelling area, bales of raw wool were conveyed through this 'taking-in' door and up a narrow internal staircase. Where the taking-in door could not be so conveniently approached then the material was hoisted up, and the wooden hoist beams sometimes still remain above the doors.

There were several variations on this basic style. Some houses do not have taking-in doors, indicating that they were built after the advent of factory carding and spinning so that the house was used exclusively for weaving, for the warps could easily be carried internally through the house. In later houses the long mullioned windows gave way to square or slightly tall sash windows sometimes arranged in pairs separated by a single mullion, an innovation which started in the dwelling portion and gradually spread to the windows of the workrooms. In some houses weaving was practised not in an upper room but in a basement usually approached internally but sometimes by an external flight of steps.

The old part of the village of Golcar has three-storey weavers' houses with ranges of mullioned window lights running almost the entire length of the front, and blocked-up taking-in doors at first floor level behind (Fig 31). Along Lumb Lane in Almondbury, another village near Huddersfield, there is a long terrace of weavers' cottages in which the upper floor windows formerly stretched almost the full length of the frontage although some have now been filled in. Wilsden near Bingley

31   Rear view of weavers' cottages at Golcar, Huddersfield, showing first-floor 'taking-in' doors now blocked or converted to windows. The frontages display long rows of mullioned window lights.

has a range of five three-storey cottages fronting on to the main street; an arched opening dated 1832 between two cottages leads through to the rear where taking-in doors can be seen. The windows are not of the long mullioned but of the later sash variety, tall and arranged both singly and in pairs. The Smallbridge district of Rochdale used to have many weavers' homes, and although most have disappeared under the bull-dozer some rows can still be found along the Littleborough road. One three-storey example demonstrates the use of sash windows for the lower dwelling quarters and retention of the older mullioned form for the upper workrooms.

In the cotton weaving villages of east Lancashire around Blackburn the weavers' cottages were quite different in style from those so far described. J.G. Timmins found that here the first or second floor loom-shop was relatively uncommon and few three-storey houses were built. Instead weaving was carried out in ground floor and basement loom-shops. In the first case the loomshop was sometimes at the rear of the dwelling quarters either as a room within the main range or as a projecting extension, but more commonly it was at the side of the living space. In many instances the side loomshop and the rooms above it have been converted into a separate dwelling disguising the original layout. This is likely to have taken place after the middle of the nineteenth century when the decay of hand-loom weaving made the old loom-shops surplus to the needs of the occupiers and sustained urbanisation maintained the demand for low-cost housing. Rows of long mullioned windows are rare, and instead the workroom was illuminated by a squarish triple or double window divided by thick mullions, or by two adjacent windows. The front door is often surmounted by a semi-circular stone arch with a keystone at the apex, the only concession to ornamentation. Frontal masonry is frequently of the dressed stone 'watershot' type in which the face of each stone block is angled so that the upper edge projects above the lower edge. Gables and rears of buildings are of uncoursed rougher blocks.

This housing type is illustrated by a row of cottages at Belthorn, a hill village between Blackburn and Haslingden. The cottages have double fronts, sometimes with two windows on the side which housed the old loomshop. Hoddlesden in the valley below has a row of cottages of varying dates and styles, some of which have cellars lit from the streets outside (Fig 32). In Blackburn itself on Manor Road there is a terrace of some thirty houses now with single frontages. At the time of building they stood in open country and are marked as the 'Long Row' on the 1848 Ordnance Survey map. It appears that these dwellings were created from perhaps ten double-fronted weavers' cottages by blocking up internal walls and converting some windows into doorways. Here the

32  Weaver's cottage, Hoddlesden, near Darwen. This row of cottages had basement workshops, each of which might have contained two or three looms. Basement workshops were very common in north-east Lancashire.

opportunity was sometimes taken during the conversion to add new doorways and higher windows reaching to the eaves. Along Limbrick, one of the oldest streets in Blackburn, a similar conversion of weavers' cottages can be seen. Not far from Manor Road at West View Place stands a colony of some fifty cottages, eighteen of which had basement loomshops and therefore required steps up to the front doorways, which have the characteristic semicircular arched heads. In 1851 the colony housed 279 people, most of the employed inhabitants being engaged in hand-loom weaving. It was one of the largest concentrations of hand-loom weavers in east Lancashire.

## Industrial housing

The most widespread type of housing in the central Pennines apart from modern post-war development is the rows of terraced houses created during the region's period of great industrial prosperity. The earliest of these houses date from around 1820 and they continued to be built until 1914. Some of the earlier ones were not greatly different in appearance from some of the weavers' cottages except that there was no specialised working accommodation. Many were built by the mill owners for their workers, the typical artisan's house having a downstairs living room with scullery and one or two bedrooms above. Better houses had a small paved yard at the rear, but others were built back-to-back with no through ventilation. Water was obtained from communal taps, and several households shared a water closet.

Social historians of the Industrial Revolution have often drawn attention to the overcrowding and poor living conditions in early industrial housing. Slum clearance in recent years has made these houses increasingly rarer, but examples still survive to show the types of conditions which existed. At Barrowford, Pendle, there are terraces of three-storey back-to-back cottages with no through ventilation, the entrance to the rear dwellings being obtained from connecting passages through the buildings. Belmont is another Lancashire village with similar types of dwelling.

The Public Health Act of 1875 laid down certain minimum standards of building and one of the most evident changes in the design of post-1875 houses it the great height of the rooms. The tall sash window with two or four large panes was now almost universal. By this time domestic building was rapidly losing its vernacular qualities as architect-designed housing became widespread. Terraced housing styles became ubiquitous, and some towns, Blackburn for example, are notable for their uniformity of housing style, although there were often marked variations in style between towns. Cheaply produced bricks began to supplant local stone in many districts; in east Lancashire the 'Accrington red' bricks gave a particularly uniform appearance to houses and mills alike. At Darwen however, in contrast to neighbouring Blackburn, stone survived as a house frontage material into the first decades of the present century.

In the deep valleys of the main Pennine axis the relief exercised considerable control over building development, and because of the steepness of slope terraces were built not alongside but on top of each other. This is most strikingly seen at Hebden Bridge. Here the hillsides are lined with terraces four storeys high. Each dwelling comprises two floors, the bottom houses fronting on to the lower hillside and the top houses on to the higher parts of the slope (Fig 4). They are a remarkable example of man's adaptation of his living accommodation to the characteristics of the physical environment.

**Selected further reading:**

R. W. Brunskill, *Illustrated Handbook of Vernacular Architecture*, Faber, 1971

T. W. Hanson, *The Story of Old Halifax*, Halifax, 1920 (reprinted S. R. Publishers, 1968)

N. Pevsner, *The Buildings of England* series. Volumes on North Lancashire (1969), South Lancashire (1969), and Yorkshire West Riding (1959). All Penguin

W. J. Smith, 'The Architecture of the Domestic System in South-East Lancashire and the Adjoining Pennines', in S. D. Chapman, *The History of Working-Class Housing*, David & Charles, 1971

C. F. Stell, 'Pennine Houses: An Introduction' *Folk Life*, vol 3, 1965

J. G. Timmins, *Handloom Weavers' Cottages in Central Lancashire*, University of Lancaster, 1977

# 7 Church and Chapel

In a secular age churchgoing is the pastime of a minority and many churches are visited more for their architectural qualities or historical associations than for their spiritual functions. Less fortunate churches unable to attract either worshippers or visitors are now often found converted to workshops or warehouses, or even derelict or demolished. This view of churches and churchgoing, however, is comparatively recent. To our forefathers the church or chapel was the most significant building in the community. Going to church occupied a large part of their rare leisure time and provided them with one of the few regular points of contact with neighbours. Spiritual comfort helped to offset their otherwise unrewarding and unending daily labours.

Churches and chapels provide much information about the communities they served. The size of a church reflects that of its former congregation, so that large churches are a sign of a once populous parish. Prosperous communities provided wealthy patrons and benefactors and so their churches are often large and lavish; but in poor communities churches were frequently small and bare. In some areas parish churches may be outnumbered by nonconformist chapels, and this in turn says something about the spiritual ethos of the community. Many churches are not the product of a single age but embody several stages of rebuilding, such extensions and alterations usually taking place at periods of population growth or increased prosperity.

In the central Pennines two religious traditions have contributed to the cultural landscape. The older is that of the established church, the origins of which lay in the organisation of society in pre-Conquest times. In medieval times this church owed its allegiance to the Pope in Rome, but during the Reformation it became the Church of England. The parishes of Anglican churches provided the basis of local government until the Industrial Revolution. In the seventeenth century the established church was joined by the nonconformist tradition which for long maintained a shadowy, furtive existence and only came into full bloom with the spread of Methodism after 1800. This tradition has given the region its many chapels. As with domestic and industrial architecture, the buildings of both traditions reflect the change from the vernacular building mode of pre-industrial times to the architect-designed styles of the factory age.

# Early parish churches and chapels

There were few churches in the Pennines before the nineteenth century and only a handful before the sixteenth century. Medieval Pennine parishes were large, each containing several townships made up of many scattered farms, hamlets, and villages. These huge parishes sometimes comprised natural units, such as the parish of Halifax, the boundaries of which are largely those of the basin of the upper Yorkshire Calder. From these great 'mother' parishes later parishes were subsequently carved.

The founding of dependent chapels had become common by the later medieval period because of the great distance of some communities from their parish church. Some were 'parochial chapels', meaning that they had full parochial rights although their chaplains were appointed by the incumbents of the mother churches. The majority, however, were 'free chapels', able to appoint their own priests, and these formed the bulk of Pennine places of workship until the nineteenth century. These chapels became full parish churches only after 1868. Halifax parish in pre-industrial times had parochial chapels at Heptonstall and Elland, both founded about 1200 to 'provide means of worship without such vast distances being involved.' In 1546 Edward VI made a survey of the free chapels of the realm with a view to confiscating their lands and rents, and the report of his commissioners is often the earliest record of the existence of these chapels. In Halifax parish the commissioners found ten free chapels, most of which had been founded early in the century when population was growing rapidly.

The original fabric of many early churches and chapels has now largely disappeared as a result of several phases of rebuilding. In the prospering industrial districts much rebuilding and refurnishing, or so-called 'restoration', took place in the nineteenth century, and modifications were invariably made in the late medieval or 'Gothic' fashion. Early 'unrestored' churches are few but some survive in remoter rural districts which escaped the wealth which went with industrial growth. Slaidburn parish church is a good example. It was founded in the late eleventh century and the oldest surviving portion is the tower, a plain square structure with angle buttresses. The interior retains its Jacobean chancel screen, traditional three-decker pulpit, and family pews each engraved with the name of the household entitled to its use. By contrast the parish church of Almondbury, despite its ancient origins, is much more a product of the Victorian age and its more substantial proportions reflect the greater wealth of the supporting community. Almondbury, now a pleasant outlying district of Huddersfield, was an important village long before the great town below it rose to prominence. The church once ministered to a parish of some 50 square miles which included Honley, Meltham, and Marsden. The chancel is the only part of the original church to survive. Internal chapels were added in the fourteenth century and the nave is of the late fifteenth century. The church then remained largely unaltered until the 1870s when major restoration included the removal of the galleries and furniture, extension of the chapels, raising of the pitch of the chancel roof, a new porch, tiling the stone floor of the nave, and embellishment of the tower and roof with battlements and pinnacles.

In many growing industrial towns of the nineteenth century the opportunity was taken to demolish the old churches in favour of completely new structures. This was the case at Blackburn, where in 1820-6 the old parish church of St Mary was almost wholly rebuilt. At Heptonstall an opportunity for rebuilding was provided fortuitously in 1847

33  Kirkburton Church. The *kirk* or church of Burton was first recorded in 1147. A *burton* was a pre-Conquest fortified farmstead. Today grass and weeds are beginning to encroach upon this ancient place of worship.

when a sudden gale tore off the church roof and it was decided to build a new church within the same churchyard. Today the Victorian Gothic structure which incorporates the old clock and bells stands side by side with the shell of the medieval church. The former towers above the roof-line of Heptonstall and dominates by its height and the splendour of its buttresses, pinnacles, and high windows, whereas the medieval church is a low, squat structure which impresses by its rugged character (Fig 34). In contrast with the clean geometrical lines of its drawing-board successor, its irregular shape and varied window styles betray a piecemeal growth over the centuries in response to the needs of its community.

## Churches of the industrial age

The nineteenth century was the principal period of Pennine church building. As industrial towns grew apace the populations of ancient parishes swelled several fold and the creation of new parishes became widespread. Consequently many towns have few or no churches which can be dated before 1800. Of Darwen's six Anglican parish churches

34 Heptonstall old church. The ruins of this medieval parochial chapel stand next to the modern church. They show that Heptonstall must have been a flourishing community in medieval times.

only one has pre-industrial origins; this is the church of St James of 1722. It stands not at the modern town centre but in an old moorside district called suitably enough Chapels, which overlooks the main part of the town by which it was long ago absorbed. Darwen's next oldest church is Holy Trinity of 1827, a product of the factory era.

From the old mother parish of Halifax twenty-seven new churches and parishes were created after 1820. Certain of these churches resulted from an Act of Parliament of 1818 which granted one and a half million pounds for the building of new churches in the industrial districts of England because of the danger to the country 'for want of places of public worship, particularly for persons of the middle and lower classes.' The populous industrial north secured the lion's share of the grant, and in the Halifax area four such 'Commissioners' churches were built. One was in Cragg Vale, a growing area of water-powered mills, two were in the new industrial towns of Hebden Bridge and Brighouse, and the fourth was in Halifax itself. Other new churches around Halifax were built by public subscription. The lists of subscribers were headed by local mill owners and other prominent industrialists, and even the Dowager Queen Adelaide appeared on the Mytholmroyd St Michael subscription list. St John, West Vale, was built in 1882 largely as a result of the efforts of the wife of the vicar of Greetland who raised the money by her skill as a needlewoman. Yet other churches were outright gifts; Colonel Edward Akroyd of Bankfield built churches on his workers' estates at Haley Hill and Copley.

The new churches were mostly built in a medieval or 'Gothic revival' fashion which attempted a return to the church building styles of the later Middle Ages, especially the Decorative and Perpendicular. Certain architects featured prominently in this revival, particularly Edmund Sharpe, E.G. Paley, and H.J. Austin. The 'Commissioners' churches, built to a budget, were sparsely finished off, but churches built in middle or upper class neighbourhoods were lavishly decorated. St Edmund, Falinge, in Rochdale, consecrated in 1873, was built at a cost of £22,000 largely at the expense of Albert Hudson Royds, a leading industrialist and prominent freemason 'at a time when a good church could be provided for half that amount'. Certain dimensions were said to be proportional to Solomon's Temple, and the roof over the chancel was described as 'a *tour de force*, faceted, columned, and panelled with bewildering complexity'. Christ Church at Walshaw, Bury, was built in 1888 at the expense of the Haworth family, cotton spinners and fustian makers, and is prominently named the Jesse Haworth Memorial Church below the huge stained glass window of the west front. It stands on a hill and its fine spire was designed to be clearly visible from the town of Bury below to the east.

# Nonconformist chapels before 1800

The established church requires a priest to interpret the Word of God to the congregation, but the essence of nonconformity is freedom of conscience or the right of each man to know God without recourse to an intermediary. Nonconformity or Dissent originated in the sixteenth century soon after the Reformation but was forced to remain underground for most of this and the following century. At this period nonconformists met for worship secretly in private houses, and only with the Act of Toleration (1689) were they allowed to erect public meeting houses or chapels.

The movement had a clear appeal to the independent-minded population of the Pennines and by 1700 was well established. It grew quickly during the eighteenth century and by 1750 there were at least as many meeting houses of Dissenters as there were Anglican places of worship. Certain districts appear to have been particular cradles of the movement (Fig 35). The moorland fringes around Chorley, Bolton, and Bury fostered the Unitarians, a group which rejected the idea of the Trinity and believed instead in the unity of Christ, and they erected several chapels in this area during the early eighteenth century. The Burnley area was another centre of nonconformity; the Quakers or Society of Friends erected a meeting house at nearby Briercliffe soon after a visit by their leader, George Fox, in 1652, while chapels at Trawden and Wheatley Lane were built by followers of Benjamin Ingham, a member of the Moravian Brethren who claimed John Hus of Bohemia as their founder. John Wesley first preached in the area in 1747, and local Methodist societies were founded shortly afterwards. In 1767 the Baptists founded a chapel at Haggate, and another in Burnley itself 20 years later.

Even after the Toleration Act there was often violent local opposition to nonconformist meetings and the building of chapels. The Reverend William Grimshaw, Anglican clergyman of Haworth, held Methodist meetings in his own kitchen until the village acquired its first chapel in 1758. Moore's history of Burnley Methodism recounts that in the same year the builder of Padiham's first Methodist preaching house deceived passers-by into thinking he was building a pair of dwellings instead. 'He built the outside walls or shell of the house first; and when anyone, noticing that there were no interior walls, asked him what he was doing he said he wanted to get the outside walls up and the slates on while the fine weather lasted as he could build the inside in the winter. When finished, it was licensed as a place of workship before it was known in the neighbourhood for what purpose it was intended.' This Old Chapel was superseded by a bigger chapel some 20 years later, and was indeed used subsequently as a dwelling house.

These early chapels and meeting houses were built to various plans but had in common a simplicity of presentation and exhibited the vernacular qualities of the domestic architecture of the period. They

35 Nonconformity in the western Pennines before 1800. Many early chapels and meeting houses were in small remote places where meetings were less vulnerable to disruption. The erection of a chapel was often preceded by several years of discreet gatherings in private houses.

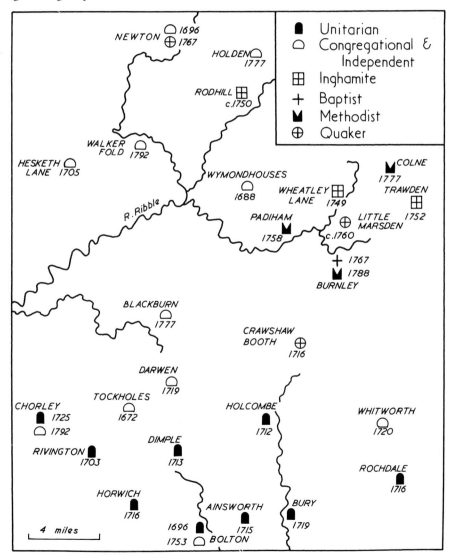

were built of coarse blocks of local sandstone and were designed by and for their congregations. Sometimes their architecture betrays little of their ecclesiastical functions — this is particularly so with the Quaker Meeting Houses which were used for secular as well as religious meetings. The Meeting House at Crawshaw Booth, Rossendale, is a square low structure which, other than for the two large transformed windows to the right of the door, might easily be passed over for a secular building. The most common shape for nonconformist chapels is rectangular, with a symmetrical frontage on one long side incorporating two doors for men and women to enter separately. The pulpit is normally located on the other long side opposite the door and faces a gallery running round three sides. The Wesleyan chapel at Greetland, built in 1777 above the busy thriving Yorkshire Calder valley conforms to this pattern although porches were added in 1897 and the original doors were replaced by windows. Some 60 years older and still in its original rural setting is the Unitarian chapel at Rivington near Chorley, its tree-shaded graveyard completing a scene that has changed little for over two and a half centuries (Fig 36).

A particularly interesting chapel plan is the octagon, personally favoured by John Wesley since 'in it the devil can find no corner in which

36 Unitarian chapel, Rivington, erected in 1703. The Unitarians erected several small chapels in the western Pennines in the early eighteenth century. Men and women entered by separate doors.

to hide' and represented by the old Methodist chapel at Heptonstall (1764). It was built of local stone and the builders were helped by many of the villagers. The roof proved too difficult for local building knowledge and so was made at Rotherham and hauled to the village by pack-horses. At Heptonstall the pure octagon shape was short-lived, for by 1802 the congregation had grown so large that the building had to be extended by lengthening two of the walls. In 1813 a Sunday-school building was added. At that time the chapel had over four hundred members, while the Sunday-school had over a thousand children, seventy-two teachers, four superintendents, and four secretaries. It was the growth of followers on this scale that fostered the proliferation of Methodist chapels throughout the Pennines during the coming century.

## Nineteenth century chapels

The nineteenth century was the great age not only of church but also of chapel building. In many parts of England and Wales where population was growing rapidly the established church failed to rise to the needs of the swelling communities, providing an opportunity for the nonconformist movements to fill the gap. The basic nonconformist doctrine that all men, regardless of their origins, could know God directly, had a powerful appeal at all levels of society but particularly amongst the new and growing industrial working classes. Unlike the established church, which was organised by a centralised episcopal hierarchy, the organisation of nonconformity sprang from the local community. In helping to build a chapel with his own labour and participating in its running by preaching or administration, many a man found responsibility and a sense of dignity which he could never otherwise have attained.

The Lancashire and Yorkshire Pennine region was one of several areas where the renewed nonconformist zeal of the nineteenth century made a significant impact on the landscape through the spread of its chapels. In the growing industrial villages and towns nonconformist, particularly Methodist, chapels far outnumber Anglican or Catholic churches. A walk around any of the older industrial districts reveals a chapel at the end of almost every street, and they were as much a part of the Victorian scene as the terraced houses, mills, and cobbled streets. In Burnley thirty-nine new chapels were erected during the nineteenth century compared with only six new Anglican and Catholic churches. The spread of chapels, however, was as much a product of the fragmentation of nonconformity as of its growth, for after the death of John Wesley in 1791 the Methodist movement suffered a succession of schisms and each branch went its own way, building its own chain of chapels. Not until 1907 were most of these branches reunited.

The chapels of the factory era are readily distinguishable from those of the previous century. The small, simple, vernacular chapels which characterised the earlier period continued to be built in the nineteenth century but mostly in poor, remote districts serving scattered communities. The new urban chapels were of larger proportions, often two full storeys high with a rectangular box-like shape matching the neighbouring cotton mills and the grid-iron plan of the streets. While some exteriors were free of decoration and ornament, the new generation of nonconformists often felt that this strictly utilitarian approach to building suggested a lack of devotion, and the adoption of distinctive styles, especially for frontages, became common. While the new generation of churchbuilders turned for inspiration to the Gothic fashion, the chapel builders utilised Classical, Renaissance, and Italianate models.

The Providence Methodist Church at Golcar near Huddersfield (1883) is typical of many larger Victorian chapels. It is a two-storey structure of grey stone, seven bays long and five wide. The middle three bays of its symmetrical facade are surmounted by a pediment containing a clock beneath which is a stone slab bearing the chapel's name picked out in large capitals. Bold corner pilasters give the illusion of supporting

37 United Reformed Church, Booth, Luddenden. The chapel is the dominating landscape feature of this small mill community. The rose window looks back to secular building styles of the seventeenth century.

the frontage and a further pair of pilasters contain the middle three bays. On the ground floor two front bays contain the doors, approached by steps flanked by parapets. The arched windows, linked by string-courses, are repeated all round the building, but otherwise the Classical styling is confined to the frontage. The building dominates the rows of terraced cottages adjoining the roadside. In Darwen the now disused Railway Road Methodist Church (1864) has an even more striking Classical facade. Here the massive pediment rests upon a broad entablature supported by giant columns enclosing a wide centre bay, and the building looks across the town centre to the hillside streets and moors beyond.

By the late nineteenth century some chapel builders were returning to the Gothic style espoused by church architects but rejected by the early nineteenth century nonconformists as insincere. There was a tendency for chapels to become lavish, both outside and inside, to resemble churches more closely, and as with the Golcar and Darwen examples given above, even to be called churches. Such a building is the square Congregational Church of Halifax (1857), described by Pevsner as 'the most ambitious church' in the centre of this town. It has a tower and spire over 200 ft high donate by Sir Francis Crossley, a wealthy industrialist. Equally commanding is the United Reformed Church at Booth, Luddenden (Fig 37). It stands on the hillside above the tiny industrial hamlet, and its magnificent frontage, with twin towers and huge rose window, dominates the narrow valley and its rows of cottages. It is one of many monuments in the Pennines to the great age of chapel building.

**Selected further reading:**

H. Braun, *Parish Churches: Their Architectural Development in England*, Faber, 1974

A. Goodwin, 'How the Ancient Parish of Halifax was Divided', *Transactions of the Halifax Antiquarian Society*, 1961

K. Lindley, *Chapels and Meeting Houses*, John Baker, 1969

B. Nightingale, *Lancashire Nonconformity*, 1890

N. Pevsner, *The Buildings of England* series. Volumes on North Lancashire (1969), South Lancashire (1969), and the West Riding of Yorkshire (1959). Penguin

# 8 Fields in the Landscape

Most people living in Britain today are town dwellers, while the majority of those who live in the countryside pursue a largely urban way of life in rural surroundings. This has been the case for only a relatively short period of time. Many people who trace their ancestry are surprised to find that their urban lineage has rural roots which lie no further back than four or five generations. Until the nineteenth century most people were directly dependent upon the countryside for their livelihood; they either farmed their own land or worked for other landowners.

Fields are the most widespread evidence of this former bond between man and the land. Fields are as man-made as houses or factories and were created to enable the land to produce more food than it would yield in its natural state. Fields were therefore created at periods of growing demand for food or of high food prices. At other times when the demand fell or when food was more cheaply obtained elsewhere fields were abandoned and allowed to revert to their natural condition. The cultivated zone of the landscape has therefore never been of constant extent but has always been growing or contracting. The fields themselves have been subjected to variations in shape and size in response to changes in farming methods.

Halifax's historian T. W. Hanson was very much aware of the contribution of fields to the Pennine landscape. Writing half a century ago, he distinguished three distinct bands in the landscape of the valleys around Halifax. The lowest zone comprised the steep wooded banks of the deeply incised streams. Above this extended the zone of farmland and settlement, giving way to the highest or moorland zone. The sequence is still recognisable in most Pennine valleys although the extent of each zone varies. Where lower slopes are gentle the 'field' zone reaches the valley floor; in other localities it may also reach the highest summits.

Pennine fields reached their greatest extent during the first half of the nineteenth century. Since then there has been a contraction in the number of fields and in their total area. Along valley floors and lower hillsides urban and industrial growth has nibbled away steadily at the cultivated area, leading to its total disappearance in many places. The upper margin of agriculture has also contracted as more and more poor quality land has proved uneconomic to farm or heads of valleys have been transformed into reservoir catchments. Mining and quarrying have often cut great scars into the field pattern, breaking it up and in some cases removing entire hillsides.

The many fields that remain provide in their shape and arrangement a wealth of information about the conditions under which they were created and the progress of the steady conversion of wilderness into farmland. Because modern farming is most conveniently carried out in large fields, walls and hedgerows have often been removed, creating new field shapes and obscuring long-established patterns. For this reason modern maps are frequently less satisfactory to consult about field patterns than older editions. The first edition six-inch maps of the Ordnance Survey published from the 1840s are an especially valuable record of former field patterns. By far the best place to study fields however is outdoors; only there can field patterns be seen in a proper scale and perspective, and the effort required in human labour to create them be fully appreciated.

## Medieval open fields

Wray-with-Botton is a very extensive parish lying on the north-western slopes of the Bowland fells overlooking the Wenning valley. North and east of the village of Wray extending towards the River Roeburn is a compact block of fields forming elongated parallel strips. At Clifton near Brighouse a similar pattern of parallel fields can be seen, containing as at Wray only a small proportion of the land of the parish but immediately surrounding the village. The pattern is repeated at many old villages along the Pennine valleys.

These fields are of variable age. Some may have been created as early as the fourteenth century, others as late as the nineteenth. Their shape, however, fossilises the earlier pattern of medieval open, common, or town fields, for each elongated field was created by the enclosure of a block of adjacent strips in the old townfield. The townfields are the oldest field type in the central Pennines and represent a system of farming now long since disappeared.

At one time it was believed that there were few or no open fields in the region, but it is now considered that most pre-Norman Pennine villages had common fields. Sometimes their existence is evident from the modern map, as in the case of the villages named above. In other cases field names survive which are indicative of former common field farming, for example *butt* (meaning an irregularly shaped parcel of the townfield) or *balk* (boundary between strips in a townfield). The common fields were restricted to Anglian settlements and are unknown in forest and other regions not settled until later medieval times. Even in Anglian villages they never occupied more than a small portion of the land of the village.

A survey of Clifton in 1788 reveals some of the principal features of Pennine common fields (Fig 38). The village by that date straggled for half a mile along a single main street. Most of the cottages lay on the northern side, backing on to small household plots or crofts (Chapter 5).

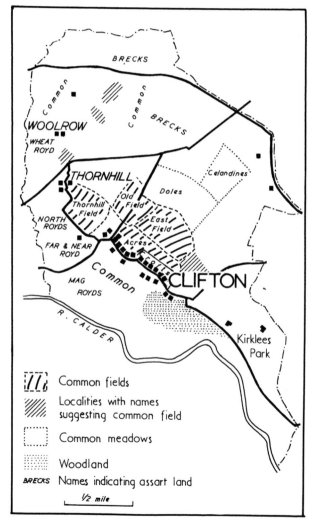

38   Fields at Clifton, an open field village in the Calder valley. Field names in a survey of the parish in 1788 show the location of old open fields, by then enclosed. Outlying fields of the parish originated as 'assart' land enclosed from the waste in later medieval times.

Beyond the crofts lay the former open fields, by that time enclosed but recognisable by the strip shape of the new fields. The nearest open field to the village was the *Acres*, once the permanent tillage or *infield* of the original settlers. Beyond the *Acres* were the *East Field* and *Old Field*, later common fields. Within the township of Clifton half a mile from the village was Thornhill, a hamlet which probably originated as a break-away colony from the main settlement and tilled its own open field. Common field names in the vicinity of Woolrow, another hamlet, suggest that this settlement also may once have had its own townfield.

At Clifton each farmer would have held not a compact block of land but scattered strips in different parts of the townfield. This fragmentation may have arisen so that each farmer would have a share of both the rich and poor land in the townfield. An alternative explanation is that when the fields were first created each farmer had a compact piece. Since at death property was normally divided between co-heirs, each son would inherit a portion of his father's land. By marriage a son might acquire a further portion elsewhere, and on his own death both parcels would be divided between his heirs. Over several generations the compact blocks would be broken down into small strips and a highly fragmented pattern of landholding would develop.

The townfields provided the arable land of the early villages. The boundary of each townfield was marked by a thick hedge or *ringyard*, but within the field there were few boundaries other than stones or posts between strips and grass headlands at the ends of strips on which the plough team could be turned. Oats was the staple crop, being the only cereal that could be grown in the damp, cool conditions. In early May animals would be driven from the townfields and common waterside meadows, where they had been wintering, to summer pasture on the moorland wastes. Oats would then be sown in the townfields and hay allowed to grow in the meadows. After haymaking and harvesting the animals would be brought down from the fells and wintered in the townfields and meadows on stubble and hay. The townfield was thus allowed the winter to recover for the next year. This is however a highly generalised picture of townfield farming, and many variations existed in farming practice and land utilisation between the townfields of neighbouring villages.

It is unlikely that the townfield area of most villages underwent much enlargement after the eleventh or twelfth centuries. Instead the emphasis changed from communal to individual farming, and most new fields created in later medieval times were of the enclosed type. Indeed, from about this time the common field farming system began to break up. As copyhold tenure became more widespread, farmers took the opportunity to amalgamate their strips into compact blocks which could then be surrounded by a hedge. These new hedges therefore outline the old pattern of strips. But even after this consolidation and enclosure holdings often remained fragmented. Clifton in 1788 had several farmers whose lands consisted of several scattered parcels long after enclosure of the common fields had been completed.

In some townships common field persisted through the eighteenth into the nineteenth century. A map of some properties in Newton (1765) shows that a number of parcels were still in the form of strips (Fig 39). At neighbouring Slaidburn strips survived late enough to be recorded on the Slaidburn Tithe Map of 1844.

## Medieval and Tudor enclosed fields

Most later medieval Pennine fields were not of the open communal type but of the more familiar enclosed design. Their dates of origin are often quite difficult to identify because these enclosed fields were created

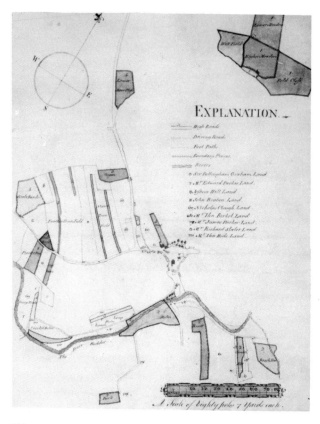

39 Estate map showing land in Newton belonging to Mr Edward Parker of Browsholme, 1765. Parts of the townfield still lay in open strips.

over a very long time span and their patterns vary not so much with period of origin as with the nature of the terrain. A common feature is their creation not by village communities but by individual farmers. Some in the upper Wyre and upper Hodder valleys were the work of tenth century Norse pioneers. Many others elsewhere were carved out of the wastes by enterprising freeholders on lands granted to them at nominal rents by their manorial lords. Around the edges of townfields are additional enclosures created by townfield farmers as a means of increasing the size of their holdings. During the fifteenth and sixteenth centuries further enclosures were made from forest lands by new colonists, while throughout the Pennine region at this period squatters filled up gaps in the settlement pattern by appropriating odd scraps of land discarded by earlier settlers.

Along the Hodder valley around Newton and Slaidburn there is much evidence of the gradual assarting of the woodland wastes. North of Slaidburn is a district called Woodhouse, now a tangle of winding lanes, footpaths, small irregularly shaped fields, and numerous dispersed farms, but until later medieval times heavily wooded. Kirkstall Abbey once had stock enclosures here, and the Abbey records mention assarting at Woodhouse in the years before 1367. About this time the farm of Shay House must have been built (the name derives from *sceaga* meaning copse), for in the fifteenth century it formed part of the endowment of Slaidburn church. By the sixteenth century Woodhouse was quite densely populated with small farms, but still had patches of waste ground which were gradually appropriated by squatters. Several farms in this district started life as squatters' cottages and still bear the names of their original occupiers, such as Procters, Myttons, Lanshaw, and Pages (Fig 40). Throughout the district there are many irregularly shaped fields providing evidence of the gradual advance of the cultivated landscape up the hillslopes.

Along the Calder valley and its tributaries between Todmorden and Brighouse there is much evidence of the creation of new hillside fields. The name *royd*, a variant of *ridding*, is especially common in this region. Clifton has its North Royd, Far Royd, Mag Royd, and Wheat Royd fields, while other Clifton fields are called *brecks*, referring to land 'broken' from the wastes. All these fields are in outlying parts of the township on former common wastes. The sixteenth century appears to have been a particularly important period in the creation of royd land in Calderdale. A commission appointed in 1565 to investigate encroachments on waste land in the Halifax region found that since 1509, 219 acres of land had been appropriated in Hipperholme and 239 acres in Sowerby. At Holmfirth further south 545 acres had been enclosed.

Hanson relates how new royd land was created from the slopes beneath the steep escarpment of Illingworth Edge north of Halifax.

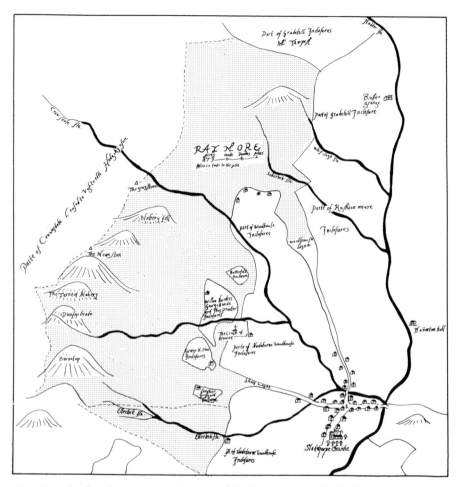

Part of gradehull Inclosures
mr Tempst

Rusfin grange

part of gradehill Inclosure

RAWMORE
acres roode Dawks perches
879    0    6    2
After 24 foote to the pole

The gragstone

Blabery fell

The Nearstone

The Tarne of Blabery

Dunsop heade

Part of Crawshale Crosse from Holly moor stone

Crawshale Stone

Inderbeck fla

Part of Rushton meare

Inclosures

part of woodhouse Inclosures

woodhouse Layne

Butterfell Inclosure

william banke george banke and John proctor Inclosures

The Croft of browne

part of Slaidburne Woodhouse Inclosures

George Hitton Inclosures

Burnslop

Casper Graham

Elterbeck fla.

Elterbeck fla

Shay Layne

pt of Slaidburne Woodhouse Inclosures

Slaidburne Churche

Haratton hall

40  Moorland reclamation north-west of Slaidburn, 1592. The hilly tract called
Rawmoor was used as common pasturing ground by the villagers of Slaidburn, but
the edge of the moor was being eaten into by the settlements of squatters, several of
whose cottages are depicted. Much of the rest of the moor was enclosed by Duchy
of Lancaster commission in 1622.

Here the ground falls sharply from the gritstone Edge to the valley 300 ft
below. Looking westwards from the Edge across the Ovenden valley
Hanson noticed the difference between the rough ground immediately
beneath the crags and the lower enclosed cultivated ground which
sloped gently down to the stream. He found that until the sixteenth
century all the land, including the lower enclosures, had been waste, but
in 1524 one William Lister was granted two acres and three roods of this
land by the lord of Ovenden manor. Lister began to prepare this land for

cultivation and grazing by clearing it of stones and boulders, breaking up the larger rocks. He used these stones to build a wall to enclose the new field. He then felled the trees, grubbed up the roots, and dug the land over. The following year he took another acre from the waste, in 1532 a rood, in 1535 three acres, and in 1542 an acre and a quarter. Over a period of eighteen years he thus added some eight acres to his farm. Altogether between 1521 and 1581 208 acres were taken from the wastes of Ovenden by farmers such as Lister.

## The Duchy of Lancaster's enclosures

The riddings and encroachments described above were the work of individual farmers, but during the sixteenth century a rather different form of enclosure began to make its mark on the landscape. In certain manors belonging to the Duchy of Lancaster estates of the Crown, tracts of moorland were enclosed by entire villages or township communities, the terms of enclosure of each piece of waste land being determined by negotiation between the township and the Crown. The waste was then partitioned between the villagers according to their respective claims upon it. This usually depended upon the number of livestock a villager had formerly been permitted by the laws of the manor to put out to pasture on the waste, which in turn depended upon the extent of his existing enclosed fields. The wealthier villagers were naturally enough the chief promoters of this form of enclosure since they stood to gain the largest share of the land. Many poorer people on the other hand gained very little from the enclosure and lost the common rights on which they were so dependent. Enclosure was particularly widespread on the moors around Burnley and Colne and in south-eastern Bowland. Much of it was accomplished between 1622 and 1630.

Apportionment of the land was accomplished by commissions appointed by the Duchy of Lancaster, each comprising a number of local gentry often assisted by a professional surveyor. The commissioners first surveyed the waste to determine its size and a map was sometimes prepared to show its location and extent and the villages which had claim upon it. The commissioners then partitioned the waste between the villagers entitled to allotments. At the division of the Slaidburn manor commons in 1621, some 3,100 hectares of moorland were divided between six villages and various other claimants. A handful of prominent landowners each gained over forty hectares of new land. Small amounts were also set aside for public roads and for the common use of poor people and squatters who were not entitled to an allotment.

This type of enclosure has left a distinctive pattern of fields. Although some allotments proved too large to work and were subdivided into smaller pieces, the fields created were generally larger than the 'riddings' made by individual farmers along the Yorkshire Calder at the same period. Around Burnley and Colne urbanisation has obscured the field pattern but it is well preserved on the moors between Grindleton and Slaidburn and to the north-west of Slaidburn. These fields are markedly more regular in shape than earlier fields, their boundaries dividing the hillsides into long strips running the length of the slope, between 70 yd and 100 yd wide, subdivided by further boundaries across the slope to produce fields of between 3 and 12 acres.

## Fields of an industrial age

The regularly-shaped enclosures created by the Duchy of Lancaster's commissioners proved to be the prelude to a much more extensive phase of moorland enclosure a century later. From about 1770 enclosure by

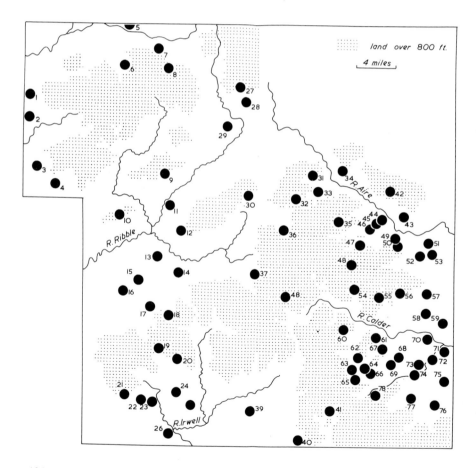

41 Enclosure by Act of Parliament.
Most Parliamentary enclosures occurred between 1770 and 1820, completing the creation of the Pennine fields. Dates are those of the Act of Parliament initiating enclosure.

| No | Township |
|----|----------|
| 1 | Quernmore, 1811 |
| 2 | Ellel, 1756 |
| 3 | Barnacre, 1771 |
| 4 | Claughton, 1730 |
| 5 | Bentham, 1767 |
| 6 | Tatham, 1853 |
| 7 | Clapham-cum-Newby, 1848 |
| 8 | Austwick, 1809 |
| 9 | Grindleton, West Bradford, Waddington, & Bashall Eaves, 1812 |
| 10 | Aighton, Bailey, Chaigeley, Dutton, & Thornley (Longridge Fell), 1808 |
| 11 | Clitheroe (Low Moor), 1786 |
| 12 | Wiswell, 1789 |
| 13 | Billington, Dinckley, & Wilpshire, 1788 |
| 14 | Clayton-le-Moors (Enfield Moor), 1794 |
| 15 | Little Harwood, 1776 |
| 16 | Blackburn, 1841 |
| 17 | Lower Darwen, 1779 |
| 18 | Oswaldtwistle, 1774 |
| 19 | Entwistle (Cranberry Moss & Aushaw Moor), 1856 |
| 20 | Edgworth, 1795 |
| 21 | Horwich, 1815 |
| 22 | Bolton, 1792 |
| 23 | Tonge, 1812 |
| 24 | Harwood, 1797 |
| 25 | Ainsworth & Radcliffe (Cockey Moor), 1809 |
| 26 | Farnworth & Kearsley (Halshaw Moor), 1796 |
| 27 | Long Preston, 1799 |
| 28 | Hellifield, 1846 |
| 29 | Halton West, 1781 |
| 30 | Barnoldswick & Salterforth (White Moor), 1814 |
| 31 | Cononley, 1768 |
| 32 | Thornton-in-Craven, 1819 |
| 33 | Glusburn, 1788 |
| 34 | Kildwick, 1848 |

| No | Township |
|----|----------|
| 35 | Keighley (Oakworth Moor), 1849 |
| 36 | Trawden, 1817 |
| 37 | Worsthorne, 1846 |
| 38 | Stansfield (Todmorden), 1815 |
| 39 | Siddall, 1812 |
| 40 | Oldham, 1802 & 1803 |
| 41 | Saddleworth, 1810 |
| 42 | Bingley & Keighley (Morton Moor), 1788 |
| 43 | Bingley (Gilstead Moor), 1858 |
| 44 | Keighley, Thwaites, & Newsholme, 1780 |
| 45 | Harden, 1847 |
| 46 | Bingley & Keighley (Leeds & Hainworth), 1851 |
| 47 | Cullingworth, 1809 |
| 48 | Keighley (Oxenhope), 1771 |
| 49 | Shipley (High Bank & Low Moor), 1815 |
| 50 | Bradford (Heaton), 1780 |
| 51 | Bradford (Idle), 1809 |
| 52 | Bradford (Bolton), 1819 |
| 53 | Bradford (Eccleshill), 1841 |
| 54 | Halifax (Warley, Saltonstall), 1848 |
| 55 | Halifax (Ovenden), 1814 |
| 56 | Halifax (Northowram), 1778 |
| 57 | Bradford (Wyke), 1813 |
| 58 | Brighouse (Clifton), 1778 |
| 59 | Hartshead, 1839 |
| 60 | Sowerby & Soyland, 1843 |
| 61 | Elland cum Greetland, 1803 |
| 62 | Barkisland, 1814 |
| 63 | Rishworth (Moselden Pasture), 1819 |
| 64 | Stainland, 1816 |
| 65 | Scammonden, 1814 |
| 66 | Huddersfield (Golcar), 1820 |
| 67 | Stainland (Old Lindley), 1807 |
| 68 | South Lindley, 1812 |
| 69 | Huddersfield (Longwood & Deanhead), 1814 |
| 70 | Bradley, 1789 |
| 71 | Huddersfield (Kirkheaton), 1799 |
| 72 | Huddersfield (Dalton), 1799 |
| 73 | Huddersfield, 1786 |
| 74 | North Crosland, 1799 |
| 75 | Kirkburton, 1813 |
| 76 | Kirkburton (Thurstonland), 1800 |
| 77 | Honley, 1782 |
| 78 | Meltham, 1817 |

Act of Parliament began to make an impact in the Pennines, creating a new generation of fields to add to the already complex landscape. Some eighty such Acts for the region were passed between 1750 and 1860, the majority deriving from the period 1770 to 1820. A handful included enclosure of old common field, but almost all related to the creation of new fields along moorland fringes, often at heights exceeding 1,200 ft (Fig 41). Parliamentary enclosure was particularly important in the Colne valley district around Huddersfield and on the moors overlooking Bradford. In Lancashire several Acts relate to enclosures from the moors between Bolton, Bury, and Blackburn. Enclosure was less important in the Bowland, Pendle, Burnley, Rochdale, Rossendale, and Hebden Bridge areas where colonisation in earlier centuries had already absorbed most of the worthwhile land.

The apportionment of each moorland between the farmers entitled to allotments is detailed in the Award attached to each Act. A specimen Award worth examination in some detail is that relating to the commons of Grindleton, West Bradford, Waddington, and Bashall Eaves, villages in the Ribble valley whose adjoining moorlands were enclosed under a single Act of 1812. The Award, dated 1819, appointed a commissioner to effect the enclosure. He could enquire into encroachments made on the moors over recent decades and confirm titles to encroachments of more than twenty years standing. Certain parts of the commons were to be set aside as watering places and as public quarries for obtaining stone for walls and buildings. Access roads were to be made. The remainder of the commons was to be divided among the landowners entitled to allotments 'according to their several and respective rights and interests'. The biggest landowners, the chief promoters of the enclosure, thus acquired the lion's share of the new land. Land was to be allocated in such a way that where possible a landowner's allotments adjoined his existing fields.

The 1819 Award was accompanied by a map showing the layout of the new enclosures. Comparison of this with later maps shows that several allotments were never enclosed but were sold soon afterwards to owners of larger adjacent allotments. The unenclosed allotments were mainly tiny portions which were not worth the cost of enclosure, particularly as small allotments required proportionately more boundary wall than larger ones. Some very large allotments were subdivided into smaller fields. Field boundaries were straight and most fields were of a rectangular shape. The enclosures were carried to the summit of the fell at 1,300 ft and five new farms were built on the reclaimed hillsides shortly after enclosure.

# The art of the dry stone waller

One of the most striking features of the Pennine landscape is the predominance of dry stone walls as field boundaries. Hedges and fences are generally restricted to the lower ground along river valleys, but on the hillsides the stone walls quickly become dominant. Even above the zone of fields walls are never completely absent, and few views on the open moors do not include a stone wall wandering across the undulating plateaux. On the lower slopes the stone walls reach down to the cottages and streets and form a backcloth to the mills and chimneys. Walls are the most suitable, indeed in some cases the only practicable, type of field boundary in districts where sour soil and heavy rain stunts the growth of quickset hedges. They afford the sheep their only protection against the heavy, often prolonged periods of rainfall.

The construction of new, and the repairing of old, walls has always been part of the Pennine farmer's regular round of work, but the amount of new walling required under the Enclosure Awards was usually well beyond the capacities of local farmers. Instead landowners, or in some cases the enclosure commissioners themselves, commonly hired wallers for this work and apportioned the cost among the allotment holders. The eighteenth and early nineteenth centuries were the heyday of the dry stone waller. During this period walling developed into a specialised trade pursued largely by itinerant gangs who moved from one enclosure job to the next. One such mason describes the typical waller as 'a blunt, manly, taciturn fellow', whose work was 'less purely mechanical than many others', demanding 'the exercise of a certain amount of judgement.'

> Accustomed to ascertain the straightness of a line at a glance, and to cast his eye along plane walls in order to determine the rectitude of the masonry, he acquires a sort of mathematical precision in determining the true bearings and position of objects.

Walling was largely a seasonal occupation carried out between spring and autumn, the wallers living rough in barns and old buildings and returning in the winter to their own cottages and small holdings. Other wallers took up the trade during slack periods in the mines.

Dr Raistrick describes in detail how a wall was constructed (Fig 42). A trench about three feet wide and several inches deep was made along the length of the ground to be walled. Large foundation stones ('footings') were laid in the trench and the gaps between them filled by smaller angular fragments. Subsequent courses were built up in two faces, one along each footing, using 'fillings' to occupy the gap between the faces. The slope or 'batter' of the wall was obtained by consistently shortening the width of each course. Every two feet or so rows of broad 'through'

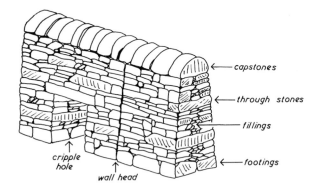

42 Some features of dry stone walling (after Raistrick).

stones were inserted across the width of the wall to give it stability. The top of the wall was finished off with cap or coping stones set across its width, the arrangement of the copings offering the waller scope for decorative features. On some walls copings are semicircular and mortared together; on others tall and shorter copings alternate; elsewhere the copings are roughly hewn and gain stability by leaning upon each other at an angle. The through stones, were inserted at regular heights and intervals, give the wall pattern and texture. Each length of wall was brought to a 'head' at openings and at points where ownership of the wall changed. Low square 'cripple' holes were provided to allow sheep to wander between fields. The cripple hole is too small for cattle and can be closed by a large flag if required.

The building of dry stone walls depended upon the availability of suitable stone. The flagstones of the Millstone Grit and Coal Measures are ideal since they split easily into regularly faced blocks, and the Enclosure Awards commonly set a field aside for a quarry for the walling. The dry stone wall landscape has both uniformity and variety. Where a single gang of wallers was responsible for an entire enclosure undertaking, the walling will be to a uniform specification; elsewhere the styles of individual wallers convey diversity and interest.

By 1840 the bulk of the walling was completed and the gangs dispersed to take up mining or railway navvying. Their fields were the last to be created in the central Pennines. In 1860 the limits of enclosed land stood higher than ever before, but many square miles of moorland still remained unenclosed. Enclosure of the moorlands was never completed and it is unlikely that it ever will be.

These last fields had pushed beyond the limits of economically cultivable ground. In many cases enclosure involved no more than a change of status for land, no improvement being made to the walled moorland grazings. Elsewhere optimistic but ill-advised farmers tried to grow corn in highly unsuitable districts such as the moors between Bolton and Blackburn, but these attempts were doomed to failure. By 1860 many of the newly reclaimed marginal lands were already reverting to moorland pasture, foreshadowing the more general desertion and depopulation of the moorlands in the present century.

## Selected further reading:

A.R.H. Baker and R.A. Butlin, *Studies of Field Systems in the British Isles,* Cambridge, 1973

W.B. Crump, 'Clifton and its Common Fields', *Transactions of the Halifax Antiquarian Society*, 1925

T.W. Hanson, *The Story of Old Halifax*, Halifax, 1920 (reprinted S.R. Publishers, 1968)

A. Raistrick, *The Pennine Walls*, Dalesman, 1969

C. Taylor, *Fields in the Landscape*, Dent, 1975

# 9  Pennine Industries

There are few parts of the Pennines where evidence of industrial activity is completely absent. Only on the highest moors of Bowland and on the central Pennine watershed does the world of factory chimneys remain wholly out of sight, but elsewhere on the moors a short walk to the nearest plateau edge invariably reveals a contrasting panorama. Gradually the ground falls away to reveal the industrial valleys with their textile mills, canals, and roads crowding into the valley bottoms and spreading on to the lower hillsides. Despite the sharp boundary between the man-made valley and the untamed moor, there is often close integration between the rural and urban elements of the landscape. Green fields extend to factory walls, mill ponds have a natural tranquility that belies their industrial origins, and rows of terraced cottages are overlooked by farmhouses. The industrial and rural faces of the Pennines complement each other and contribute to the region's distinctive character.

## Mining and quarrying

The most intensively worked mineral of the Pennines is coal. A once continuous cover of coal across the region was long ago folded upwards along a north to south axis and then planed off by the weather and rivers to expose the hard underlying Millstone Grit down the centre of the fold leaving the Coal Measures only along the eastern and western flanks. Another upfold across Rossendale likewise split the western portion of the Coal Measures into the larger south Lancashire and smaller Burnley coalfields.

These Coal Measures contain a great many coal seams, most of which are thin and discontinuous. The coal-bearing regions have nevertheless been extensively worked, although in many places little evidence of this remains on the ground. Further occasional seams occurring in the Millstone Grit have been worked in north Lancashire on the moors above Caton, Wray, Tatham, and Quernmore.

In the windswept Pennine countryside where timber was in short supply it is reasonable to assume that the heating value of coal was recognised at an early period. As early as 1308 one Richard the Nailer received permission from the lord of Wakefield manor to mine coal in Hipperholme. Population growth in the sixteenth century coupled with the increased demand for fuel for lime burning and cloth bleaching led to coal mining becoming more widespread, and by the eighteenth century the coal-bearing areas were well covered with coal pits. Defoe commented upon the wisdom of nature in placing coal seams high upon the hills so that 'the horses which fetch the coals go light up the hill and come loaden down.'

Compared to the giant collieries of today, early mines were no more than scratches on the surface of the ground, each being worked by only a handful of men. The usual method of organisation was for a coal owner to let his workings and equipment to a contractor who paid his colliers according to the amount of coal recovered. The colliers extracted the coal in two ways. In the 'outcrop working' method the miner first identified the outcrop of a coal seam along the hillside. He then drove a 'drift' or gallery along the seam, quarrying inwards until ventilation became inadequate. By making a second drift to join the first at an angle he could obtain the necessary circulation of air. Where the drift followed a seam downslope the collier ultimately found himself working in several feet of water. To overcome this a sough (drainage tunnel) was driven below the drift to meet it at a suitable low point and drain the water into a nearby stream. According to one historian soughs were made with some care: 'The great art of driving a sough was to plan it in such a way that no adjoining coal owner could possibly derive any advantage from it'. The entrance to drifts was marked by day holes, often with stone arches around their entrances.

The second method of mining involved sinking shafts or pits from the ground into the seam. Such pits were often no more than twenty yards deep and from the foot of the shaft the miner worked outwards creating a rectangular pattern of roads or 'stalls' separated by pillars of coal to support the ground above. By this method the collier could work about fifty yards from the shaft but only about half the coal could be extracted. There was always the temptation to mine coal cheaply by widening the stalls at the expense of the pillars, with the risk of collapse of the ceiling.

Early mining equipment was primitive. Coal was dug with wooden shovels edged with iron, and was drawn along passages on corves or wooden tubs without wheels. It was hauled to the surface in buckets drawn up by a simple winding gear and dragged away from the colliery on horse-drawn wooden sledges. During the eighteenth century winding was made more efficient by the introduction of the horse gin or whim, a device by which the coal was hauled up by a horse treading a circle round the pithead to turn a revolving drum around which the cable was wound. Tramroads replaced some trackways for haulage. Mechanical pumping also appeared, at first using water power, later using the Newcomen steam engine.

The first edition six-inch Ordnance Survey maps of the 1840s show the location of many early coal workings. On the moors between Darwen and Bolton there was a scatter of coal pits often no more than 100yd apart. An intricate network of tracks linked the pits to the principal roads. The maps also mark the sites of old air shafts and engine houses in the area (Fig 43).

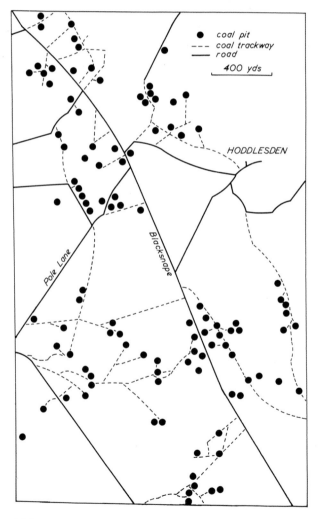

43   Coal pits on Darwen Moors, 1844. Overgrown mounds of spoil are now all that remain of the many tiny coal pits which once littered the coal-bearing rocks of the western Pennines.

Walter Bennett describes in detail a coal mine near Plumbe Street, Burnley. The shaft, sunk in 1720, was 16yd deep, and a 25yd-deep drainage shaft was sunk some 40yd away. At the top of the drainage shaft a waterwheel drove an endless chain of buckets which drew water from the shaft bottom. There were two goyts or races, one to bring water 160yd from the Calder to work the waterwheel, the second to take both wheel water and mine water 90yd back to the Calder. Coal was drawn up the main shaft by a horse whim. In 1770 this pit produced 15 to 18 tons weekly.

In the nineteenth century the vastly increased demand for coal and the introduction of the steam engine for more efficient pumping and winding stimulated the sinking of ever deeper shafts, and coal mining became a major employer in many Pennine towns. In Oswaldtwistle, where coal mining has been extinct since 1925, the industry once provide work for over a thousand people at twenty-five major colliery sites as well as many minor workings. Early mining tapped only the shallow Upper Mountain or Old Robin seam, but by 1840 many of these old workings were already abandoned and the Simpson company was quarrying the deeper Lower Mountain seam at a depth of some 200ft. Some of the older pits survived as air shafts for the compay's large Aspen and Town Bent collieries. By 1870 the industry had reached the limits of its development in the central Pennines; the shallow seams were becoming exhausted, and thenceforth the impetus lay with the larger deeper collieries then being sunk to tap the thick rich seams of south Lancashire and the plain of Yorkshire.

Physical remains of coal mining are becoming scarcer as the National Coal Board clears away abandoned workings. On the moors mounds of spoil now overgrown with vegetation indicate the position of early and long abandoned workings. In urban areas however spoil heaps have largely been quarried away and sites relandscaped, as for example at the former Bank Hall colliery in Burnley, closed only in 1967. Former shafts now often carry concrete plugs.

Remains of colliery transport are sometimes more visible. Small, early collieries were approached by tracks or roads, hence 'Coal Pit Lane' sometimes appears as a road name. Such an old road crosses the moors of Middop from Colne to the lime-burning country of Craven; another in Rossendale climbs from Shaw Clough to old pits on the moors west of Bacup. Tramroads later became common; these were narrow ways usually made of stone blocks on which iron rails were laid. The wheeled tubs carrying the coal were hauled along the rails manually or by horses. The alignment of old tramroads can often be traced from surviving bridges, cuttings, and embankments. One example is the mile-long tramroad from Sough Lane colliery in Oswaldtwistle to coke ovens at Knuzden Brook. The remains of this tramroad include an embankment and collapsed tunnel.

Stone quarrying has wrought extensive landscape changes. The most favoured stones for quarrying were the coarse sandstones of the Millstone Grit Series, so-called because of their early use as grinding stones in corn mills, but similar sandstones occurring in the Lower Coal Measures were also quarried. Extensively worked rock beds include the Haslingden Flags of Rossendale, which has a long line of large quarries along its outcrop from Musbury near Haslingden through Ewood Bridge and Brandwood to Facit, and the Rough Rock and Elland Flag sandstones of Yorkshire, from which much of the fabric of Huddersfield and Halifax was constructed. Throughout the central Pennines however there are a great many small local quarries or 'delphs'. The industry was in its heyday in the last two decades of the nineteenth century. Since then brick and concrete have supplanted stone as the chief building material, and the legacy of the industry is to be found only in the many abandoned workings.

North of the Rossendale uplands in Bowland and Craven, limestones outcrop at the surface and have been quarried very widely, but mostly on a small scale. Lime was used in medieval times for land improvement and making mortar, but with the moorland enclosure movement in the late eighteenth and early nineteenth centuries the demand greatly increased and a multitude of small quarries were opened up. Lime was an important canal traffic and its availability exerted a considerable influence on the route chosen for the Leeds and Liverpool Canal. The canal had direct access to some large quarries; at Rain Hall Rock near Barnoldswick a branch of the canal cuts directly into the limestone outcrop forming a quarry half a mile long and some 80ft deep. At Skipton another branch was built to the Earl of Thanet's quarries behind the castle.

The limestone was reduced to lime by burning in kilns often adjoining the quarry. A kiln comprised a hollow stone tower with a grate and arched opening at the bottom, and was often built into the quarry side so that it could be loaded at the top from the level. Since the limestone belt is not coal-bearing, coal for firing usually had to be brought several miles, but once a kiln was in operation it could be kept working continuously for several weeks. The 1846–51 six-inch Ordnance Survey maps show a wide distribution of kilns, many of which still survive. Most farms in the limestone belt had their own kilns, while others clustered along the towpath of the Leeds & Liverpool Canal, particularly between Skipton and Bradford where some forty kilns were erected in the 1770s.

Metallic minerals do not occur widely in the central Pennines but remains of small-scale workings can be found, mostly dating from pre-industrial times. Ironstones occur within the Coal Measures and were smelted at Low Moor near Bradford, at Colnebridge near Huddersfield, and at Newchurch in Rossendale. The Duchy of Lancaster had lead mines on Thieveley Pike in Cliviger in the seventeenth century. Bowland has remains of old lead and silver workings near Newton at Ashnott and Moor End which were being worked at least as early as the sixteenth century. Working continued well into the nineteenth century, for in 1844 these mines were leased by the Towneley family to Watkins and Innes, lead merchants, who were permitted to work and dress the ore in return for giving a ninth share of the smelted ore to the lessors. A nearby stream called Smelt Mill Clough indicates the position of a former smelting mill associated with the workings. Four miles away in the Trough of Bowland a row of houses called Smelt Mill Cottages marks the site of another old lead mine.

## Water corn mills

Water provided the power for several industries which have left a legacy of various types of small mills. One of the earliest of these industries was corn milling. Because of the mainly pastoral nature of farming comparatively less corn was ground than in many other parts of Britain, and the scattered nature of many farming communities meant that each corn mill served only a small group of farmers. Pennine corn mills were therefore small and widely dispersed. While many mill sites have medieval origins, the buildings themselves commonly date from the eighteenth or early nineteenth century when much corn was grown as a consequence of the high demand for flour.

In the more settled and industrialised zones old mills were often demolished or converted for other uses during the nineteenth century, so that corn mills most frequently survive in the rural areas. In Bowland, an area undisturbed by the Industrial Revolution, almost thirty sites of former corn mills can be identified. Some of the larger farms had their own mills, and all were located on, or close to, fast-flowing streams.

Surviving mill buildings are usually of two to three storeys. The upper storey was used for grain storage. From here grain was fed into hoppers for grinding between pairs of stones on the lower floor. The lower (bed) stone was sunk into the floor while the upper (runner) stone was driven through gearing from the great water wheel. Old corn mills are readily identifiable by the pit which contained the wheel, and the size of the pit gives some indication of the wheel's dimensions. Sometimes the wheel was of the undershot type in which the water flowed beneath, but such wheels were common only on the larger rivers with gentle gradients. On the steeper Pennine streams the overshot wheel was more usual (Fig 44); in this case the water was brought to just beyond the crest of the wheel which was turned by the power of the falling water. Water was supplied from a dammed mill pond fed by a race from a weir across the stream. The dam provided a 'head' of water, and hence more power than could be obtained from the normal flow of the stream.

The Castle Mill at Quernmore near Lancaster is a good example of a corn mill. It has ancient origins and was marked on Yates' map of 1786. The most recent building was constructed in 1818, and the mill worked until 1951. The waterwheel, 36 ft in diameter, is still intact and is of the overshot type supplied by a wooden trough. A stone wall protects the outer wheel face. The mill pond, now cloaked by trees, is on a slope above the hill and is fed by a race originating on the Conder some 500 yd from the mill. At Slaidburn the wheel has been replaced by a turbine and the mill is now used for timber sawing. The wheel pit is much overgrown but the shaft which held the wheel is visible. Bashall in the Ribble valley once had a mill which served the old hall and perhaps the long deserted medieval village nearby. The mill has been demolished but the pond and its 600 yd race can still be seen.

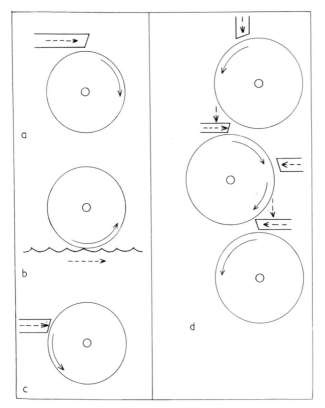

44 Types of waterwheel (after Binns):
(a) overshot
(b) undershot
(c) high breast
(d) triple waterwheels formerly at Lumbutts Mill, Todmorden.

a

b

c

d

During medieval times the corn mill played an important role in the economic life of the parish. The mill was the possession of the manorial lord and each tenant was obliged to have his corn ground at the lord's mill so that the lord could gain the revenue from the milling. In Pennine parishes, where corn yields were low, the same applied to corn brought in for sale. In the large parish of Halifax, which had about twenty-five manorial mills in the early seventeenth century, the demand for flour encouraged the building of private mills to compete with manorial mills. The manorial lords struggled hard to preserve their monopoly of milling through actions in the courts, and the costs of litigation considerably offset the income from the mills.

After 1840 local corn milling experienced a general decline as an influx of cheaper imported grain led to the eclipse of corn growing in the Pennines. The small water mills of the countryside were replaced by larger steam-powered mills at the main ports.

## The textile trade: scribbling and fulling

Two branches of the early woollen textile industry also carried out in small water-powered mills were scribbling and fulling. Scribbling was one of the earlier stages in woollen cloth manufacture in which the fibres were separated by carding and slubbing ready for spinning. Mechanisation of scribbling originated with the invention of the mechanical carder by Arkwright in 1775. The first small carding machines were operated by hand, but it was not long before larger machines were built needing water power. Some were placed in fulling mills to share the power source, but by 1800 scribbling mills themselves were becoming widespread, particularly in the Huddersfield area where the woollen trade began to centralise after other Pennine districts specialised in cotton or worsted products. Crump and Ghorbal, in their *History of the Huddersfield Woollen Industry*, counted fifty-four mills along the Colne and its tributaries in 1772 and estimated that there may have been double that number by the end of the century.

Fulling was a later stage in the woollen cloth making process. In fulling the newly woven cloth was thickened by being pounded under water prior to scouring and cleaning. Originally the process was carried out by trampling underfoot, hence the common name 'walk mill' for a fulling mill, but man-power was later replaced by water power driving wooden hammers or stocks. Until the seventeenth century there were few fulling mills and they were mostly located in the main towns. In the western Pennines early fulling mills existed at Burnley, Colne, Rochdale, and Slaidburn. In Tudor times Rossendale weavers had to carry their cloth to Rochdale for fulling, but as the woollen trade developed

45   Old worsted mill at Dolphinholme, Lancashire, built about 1784. Early mills such as this were built in rural surroundings.

fulling mills were erected in Rossendale itself. By 1750 Rossendale had seven fulling mills and this had grown to twelve by the time that Baines' *Directory* of Lancashire was published in 1825.

With the invention in 1840 of the rotary fuller which could easily be incorporated into the structure of the weaving mills, fulling mills began to fall into disuse. Some formed the sites for larger spinning or weaving mills, while others disappeared altogether in areas where cotton replaced wool. An outstanding surviving example is the Higher Mill at Helmshore near Haslingden, now being restored to working order (Fig 46). This mill, erected in 1789, is a three-storey structure with thick stone walls and timber beams. Its 17 ft diameter waterwheel is the third on the site and produced power until 1954. It formerly drove two pairs of fulling stocks, one pair of which is dated 1820.

### The textile trade: spinning, weaving, and finishing

Without doubt the mills associated with the main processes of the textile trade are the most impressive feature of the Pennine industrial scene and a major element in the landscape. The period of the textile industry's greatest prosperity was also the region's most populous period, and the mills contributed more to the growth of Pennine communities than any other single landscape feature. Although the mills spill out on to the plains on either side of the Pennines, it is nevertheless in the valleys that they dominate the scenery. This is a result not only of their physical size but also of the juxtaposition of massive sandstone architecture against steep moorland stopes. The effect is most striking where mills and their villages straggle along deeply cut valleys.

The mills of the spinning branch of the trade are physically the most impressive. Mechanisation of spinning began after about 1770 with the invention of the Spinning Jenny and Water Frame, but only really got under way with the development of Crompton's Spinning Mule in 1779. By 1800 powered mules with four hundred spindles were being built and spinning began to move from the home to mills using the new machinery. This first phase of mill development, from about 1780 to 1820, began in the cotton districts of the Lancashire Pennines, later spreading into

46   Fulling stocks at Higher Mill, Helmshore. The hammers of the stocks mechanically reproduce the ancient fulling technique of treading the cloth. These stocks pounded the cloth at thirty-nine beats per minute, taking a whole working day to full a thirty-yard piece. After fulling and scouring the cloth was stretched out to dry in the open air on tenter frames.

Yorkshire. The mills required water power sites and were therefore built along the fast-flowing streams which crossed the moorland edges. It has been estimated that a stream 3ft wide and 6in deep flowing at 3mph and turning a waterwheel 11ft in diameter can generate 5hp, which is quite sufficient to operate a small mill. These mills used the high breast type of wheel which gradually superseded the overshot wheel after 1750. Water falls from above but on the approach side of the wheel, turning it in the reverse direction to the overshot wheel.

In some localities the clustering of mills along streams was nothing short of remarkable. Along the five-mile Cheesden valley north-west of Rochdale there were in 1848 no fewer than ten spinning mills and four print works. This valley, now almost deserted, once housed a busy industrial community, and the foundations of workers' houses can be found beside the old mill ponds and mill ruins. West of Halifax the tributaries of the Yorkshire Calder cascade down fierce winding gradients into the main stream and mill sites utilise every available space. The Caty Well and lower Luddenden Brooks descend 900ft to the Calder in less than four miles, in the space of which they once powered ten mills. One mill still operating in this valley is the Jowler Mill built about 1812. In 1933 it was converted to turbine operation but this finally broke down in 1967 when the mill pond was drained. Lumbutts Mill near Todmorden was once driven by a series of three overshot wheels arranged in vertical sequence so that each wheel had its own feed but was also driven by the water falling from the wheel above it (Fig 44). The top water fell a total distance of 90ft and the system was capable of generating 54hp.

These mills were mostly small and frequently demonstrate vernacular building traditions. Like the farmhouses of the period they use local stone and harmonise with the landscape. A very early mill is the Dolphinholme Mill in the Wyre valley near Lancaster, built about 1784. This was the first water-powered worsted spinning mill and supplied yarn to weavers around Halifax and Bradford. It is built of roughly cut stone and has windows with small square panes. Timber beams support the floors.

By 1820 steam power was beginning to supersede water power, and a second phase of mill development extending to the end of the century began along the lower river valleys and canals of the coalfields where coal was easily obtained but where water was still available for washing and raising steam. Mill building in the Yorkshire Pennines was particularly pronounced along the Calder east of Todmorden and the Aire east of Keighley, and in Lancashire along the Irwell and Calder rivers and the Rochdale Canal, but few lower Pennine valleys were wholly free of the new mill development. These later mills are quite different from the

47 Cowpe Mill, Rossendale. Moorlands provide a setting for this nineteenth-century cotton mill.

earlier ones. They are larger, often four or five storeys, and commonly have a rectangular shape with a flat roof. Cast iron replaced timber for columns and beams and by the end of the century brick and terra cotta had replaced stone even in districts where it was readily available locally, particularly in east Lancashire. As larger machines and higher speeds demanded more light, windows became larger and by 1900 glass comprised a large proportion of the external structure of new mills. The basically austere design was sometimes offset by decoration on cornices, mill chimneys, and particularly on the water towers which themselves form a striking part of the structure. These later mills frequently draw upon Italianate architectural features, especially in the use of square campanile towers.

Cowpe Mill, Rossendale, is a good example of a Lancashire mill with a country setting (Fig 47). It was a fulling mill in 1825 and a woollen mill in 1844. Architecturally it is plain and functional; the spinning block is a two-storey square structure and the windows are tall with many small panes and arched tops. By contrast the mill at Denholme, built in 1851, bears external ornamentation and attempts to achieve some architectural character. It is of five storeys under one gable with eaves and cornices supported on corbels. One gable end has a circular window under the eaves. At each end of the building there is a square tower, one of which also houses a 'town hall' type of clock and is surmounted by an open parapet. There is another fine decorative square section tower at the Nutclough Mill, Hebden Bridge. The mill at Facit, Rossendale, reflects the style of later mills. Its red brick contrasts vividly with the yellow sandstones quarried on the hillside nearby, and most of the exterior comprises tall windows extending the full height of each floor; the only decoration is around the top of the leaded dome on the water tower. Among mill chimneys the 303ft high India Mill chimney, Darwen, is notable (Fig 48). It is in the form of a Venetian campanile with mock windows in the sides and base and Renaissance ornamentation at the top, and is supported on a single block of stone which required

48   The India Mill chimney dominates the skyline of Darwen. The chimney, completed in 1867, took fourteen years to build and cost twelve thousand pounds. Mock windows in the sides imitate the Campanile of St Mark's Square in Venice.

thirty-five horses to move it. Not far from the chimney is now displayed a horizontal steam engine of the type formerly used at the mill.

In the weaving branch of the cotton trade domestic manufacture persisted well into the nineteenth century, and it was not until 1840 that power weaving began to supersede the hand loom. At first, power weaving was carried out on the ground floors of the spinning mills, but by the later nineteenth century separate single storey weaving sheds were widespread. These sheds are recognisable by their roofs comprising rows of steeply inclined north-facing lights separated by more gently angled slated portions. They are particularly common in the towns of north-east Lancashire around Blackburn and Burnley where cotton weaving became a regional specialism.

The finishing branches of the industry—bleaching, dyeing, and printing—remained tied to water sources long after spinning had moved away from water powered sites. This was because of the large quantities of pure water needed. In Lancashire there was a concentration of early bleachworks and dyeworks in the Irwell valley and its northern tributaries around Bolton. Further north calico printing developed in the Oswaldtwistle and Accrington areas. Robert Peel developed block printing in Oswaldtwistle around 1760 and a number of printworks were built in the area in the years following. One of the most extensive printworks was at Broad Oak, Accrington, established about 1782. Here along the Warmden Brook a complex of dye houses, bleach houses, and print shops stretched for more than half a mile. Seven water wheels supplied power for the various hammers, rollers, and mangles and the cloth gradually moved downstream from one building to the next. The owner of the works in the nineteenth century, Thomas Hargreaves, built himself a mansion on a hill overlooking the works, and its grounds are now a public park.

**Selected further reading:**
O. Ashmore, *The Industrial Archaeology of Lancashire*, David & Charles, 1969
E. Baines, *Account of the Woollen Manufacture of England*, Published in 1858 (with a new introduction by K. G. Ponting, David & Charles, 1969)
G. R. Binns, 'Water Wheels in the Upper Calder Valley', *Transactions of the Halifax Antiquarian Society*, 1973
D. H. Holmes, *The Mining and Quarrying Industries in the Huddersfield District*, County Borough of Huddersfield, 1967
A. Raistrick, *Industrial Archaeology*, Paladin, 1973

# 10 Crossing the Pennines

Even though they stand athwart the main trunk of England, the central Pennines have never presented a serious obstacle to traffic. Unlike the mountains of Lakeland or Wales, where deep valleys terminate in steep headwalls surmountable only by winding passes, Pennine valleys lead up on to gently undulating plateaux which provide fairly level, although sometimes boggy, surfaces for routeways. Early tracks preferred these upland routes, and their growth was associated with the development of the hillside communities they served.

With the Industrial Revolution economic activity moved down into the valleys and the communication pattern shifted likewise. Along the deeply incised Walsden gorge, cut at the end of the Ice Age by escaping meltwater, a turnpike road, a canal, and a railway all struggle for space within a few yards of each other. All three were created to serve the advancing tide of industry. Sowerby Bridge on the Yorkshire Calder was a product of the same transport revolution.

The latest trans-Pennine route, the M62 motorway, dominates the scenery of the central Pennines and its path shows scant regard for the relief which influenced earlier routes. It swings across plateau and valley alike, a constant reminder of man's impact upon the physical landscape.

## Green tracks and packhorse roads

Roads depend on trade. There was probably very little trade between prehistoric Pennine communities, and so pathways never became used regularly enough to be called roads. The roads built by the Romans were for military purposes and were of only limited use to the small Celtic settlements of the time. When the Romans withdrew, their roads fell into disuse and many stretches have wholly disappeared from the landscape. An exception is the Blackburn to Bury road, regular use of which has survived to the present day.

Early medieval settlements were largely self-sufficient, each village producing the commodities which it needed for its own subsistence, but the growth of markets and fairs is evidence of the gradual development of trade during the medieval centuries. Besides larger markets such as Skipton and Clitheroe, there were also many smaller, local markets. Networks of trackways developed to link markets with surrounding villages and hamlets. The livestock rearing enterprises of the great lords in east Lancashire and the Halifax area meant that herds of cattle often had to be moved considerable distances, the cattle of the Lacy lords being sent as far afield as Norfolk for fattening. The monasteries were supplied with grain and meat from their demesne farms. All this contributed to the growing volume of traffic, so that by the end of the medieval period the Pennines were becoming well covered by a network of unpaved or 'green' tracks.

Certain routes were closely associated with the traffic of particular commodities. Lime, essential for making mortar and for the improvement of newly broken sterile land, was in short supply in many districts but was readily obtainable from limestone hillocks or 'knolls' in the Clitheroe area. From quarries in this district an old lime road or *limersgate* led across Pendle into the Calder valley and up on to the Rossendale fells. It then avoided the Rossendale valleys and instead followed the ridge of high ground to the east of Bacup and Whitworth. Along this route lime was transported to the Rochdale area on trains of packhorses. Another source of lime was glacial-strewn limestone boulders on the moors between Trawden and Hebden Bridge, from which limestone was carried along tracks down into Calderdale. This traffic continued into the nineteenth century, for as late as 1856 an artist sketching on the moors near Halifax noted that 'droves of packhorses cross these hills frequently with lime.'

Other roads were used by packhorses carrying salt northwards from the Cheshire salt-producing districts. These former saltways are recognisable by the occurrence of *salt* names at points along them. One such saltway or *saltersgate* went from Northwich to Manchester, whence it continued northwards into Tottington, crossing a *saltersbridge* on the old boundary of Holcombe Forest. The saltway then went via Pickup Bank and Oswaldtwistle, entering Great Harwood at Saltersford and continuing across Whalley Nab to Whalley and the salter's ford or *salford* just outside Clitheroe at Pendleton Brook. Salt was carried through Clitheroe in the vicinity of Salt Hill and then across the Forest of Bowland to Dunsop Bridge. From here an old road follows the Whitendale valley and then descends into Roeburndale by way of Salter Fell, Higher Salter, High Salter, Mid Salter, and Lower Salter. Such *salters* may have been salter-erghs or shelters for salt merchants.

Packhorse traffic was far more common than wheeled traffic since trains of packhorses could climb the moorland edges easily and directly. By the sixteenth century the volume of packhorse traffic was considerably swollen by the growing trade in wool and cloth. The scale of this trade is shown by the fact that in one week alone in 1569 a certain Dean Nowell was able to acquire 2,450 yd of cloth from some thirty traders or chapmen, nearly all of whom lived in the Blackburn, Whalley and Burnley districts. We can well imagine that in bad weather the continuous trains of chapmen's ponies churned the green tracks into impassable rivers of mud, and it was undoubtedly the increase in trade which led to the conversion of many heavily used tracks into paved *causeways* by laying great stone blocks or flags along their length. These causeways were narrow, usually wide enough for only one train of packhorses, and needed constant maintenance. In 1640 the accounts of the Sowerby constables included the cost of 'laying six hundred causey stones between Sowerby and Soyland' on the Halifax to Blackstone Edge road. Some causeways were improved and paved by charitable bequests. One John Holdsworth of Blackledge in Halifax left 3s 4d for mending the highway between his house and the market place.

The earliest bridges along these roads were of the 'clapper' type comprising flagstones spanning stone piers built in the stream, but by the mid-sixteenth century new arched bridges were becoming widespread. In 1514 John Hanson bequeathed money for the repair of the bridge at Brighouse, and forty years later his son left money for building a new bridge. Sowerby Bridge was rebuilt in the 1530s and Elland Bridge in 1579. On the other side of the Pennines Sir Richard Shireburn of Stonyhurst in 1562 paid one Roger Crossley seventy pounds to build across the Hodder a new bridge 'of stone substantial and surely wrought in all points' with 'four arches plain wrought and double bound and in every angle sufficient.' The bridge, now a picturesque ruin superseded by a more modern bridge upstream, was clearly not built to the intended design for it has three arches, not four (Fig 49). It has no parapets and is only 7 ft wide.

During the eighteenth century the packhorse road system reached its greatest extent. Jefferys' map of Yorkshire (1772) reveals a network focused on Halifax, the great cloth centre. From Halifax the *Via Magna* wound its way up on to Beacon Hill and went via Hipperholme to Wakefield. Westwards the road from Halifax avoided the Calder valley bottom and instead clung to the hillside, joining together the ancient townships of Warley, Luddenden, Midgley, and Heptonstall, before crossing the moors to Burnley. The remains of several old stone crosses mark the latter part of this route. Another important cross-Pennine route was from Halifax to Rochdale via Sowerby, Soyland, and

49   Lower Hodder Bridge, built in 1562, spans the Hodder a short distance above
its confluence with the Ribble. Like many packhorse bridges it had no parapets.

Blackstone Edge. An alternative route to Rochdale wound along the
hillsides south of the Yorkshire Calder by way of Erringden and
Mankinholes, and after crossing the Walsden valley climbed up on to
Ramsden Hill, where the modern Ordnance Survey map marks it as a
*Long Causeway*. This road then descended into Rochdale via Wardle.

In Pennine Lancashire Haslingden was a packhorse route focus of
importance and from it radiated several routes now long fallen into
disuse (Fig 50). From Haslingden the *King's Highway* crossed the moors to
High Riley and Huncoat, avoiding the larger settlement of Accrington.
From Huncoat the track led via the ancient churches at Altham and
Whalley to the market place at Clitheroe. Southwards another old road
climbed the moors above Holcombe to the Pilgrim's Cross just below
Bull Hill. From here it descended into Affetside where there was
another cross, and so reached Bolton by way of Tonge Moor. Yet
another important route was that westwards through Grane to Pickup
Bank, and then by Tockholes to the port of Preston.

The packhorse era drew to an end with the wane of the eighteenth
century. By that time the turnpikes were providing the basis of the

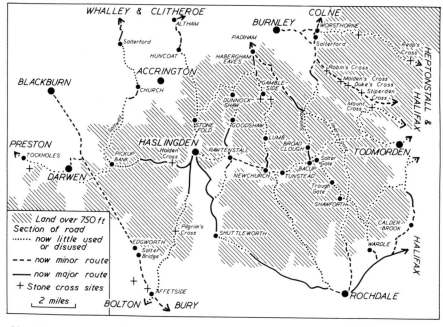

50 Disused roads in the western Pennines. A selection of old and now mostly little used routes which were the arteries of Pennine trade before the Industrial Revolution.

modern road network. Some packhorse routes were absorbed into the new system; others fell into disuse and reverted to green tracks and footpaths, which in some cases have disappeared from the modern map. Those which remain in the landscape are the fossilised arteries of an economic system long past.

## The turnpikes

Until the eighteenth century there was probably very little wheeled traffic in the Pennines, but the development of industry made it essential for larger quantities of goods to be moved quickly and easily. In 1735 an Act of Parliament was passed for 'repairing and widening the road from the town of Rochdale... leading over a certain craggy mountain called Blackstone Edge... and from thence to the towns of Halifax and Elland'. In 1741 further Acts were passed providing for road improvements from Leeds and Wakefield to Halifax. These roads were the first Pennine turnpikes.

The turnpike era ushered in a new concept in road building and maintenance. Previously road repairs had been the responsibility of the parish, which normally discharged the duty indifferently, but the Turnpike Acts provided for the setting up of trusts of men with a vested interest in road improvement. They were usually merchants, manufacturers, landowners, local officials, and indeed any persons of substance who stood to gain from better roads. Each Turnpike Trust undertook to improve and maintain its stretch of road and was empowered to charge tolls to travellers for the use of the thoroughfare.

The Pennine turnpike network grew rapidly in the late eighteenth and early nineteenth centuries in step with the development of the textile industry. Periods of especially rapid growth were the 1750s, from 1790 to 1810, and the 1820s. The pattern of roads reflected the growth of manufacturing districts; in east Lancashire the network was especially concentrated around Blackburn, Bolton, Burnley, Rochdale, Oldham, and Manchester. By contrast the Forest of Bowland, with no industrial development, had no turnpike roads.

The turnpike network reflected a basic change in the pattern of economic activity. Until the eighteenth century most manufacturing was carried out in the hillside hamlets served by the packhorse roads, but the turnpikes followed the shift of industry into the valleys. This change in route patterns sometimes took place in stages. Early turnpikes were often old packhorse routes improved and widened, and these first turnpikes were in turn replaced by lower, easier, routes. The change is seen on the roads from Blackburn to Whalley. The Whalley Old Road from Blackburn climbs by way of Little Harwood to a summit point near New Inn and then passes over the hill to descend by Whalley Nab. This was the ancient route, turnpiked by an Act of 1796. The Whalley New Road however, built after 1819, takes a lower route via Langho and Billington. It superseded the Old Road, which is now little used. Similarly there are two turnpike roads along Rossendale. An Act of 1789 empowered the Haslingden and Todmorden Turnpike Trust to maintain a road between Haslingden, Rawtenstall, Newchurch, and Bacup. This road clings to the slopes 200 ft above the upper Irwell valley and supersedes a packhorse road via Oakenhead Wood and Tunstead at a still higher level. In 1815 the same trust obtained an Act to construct a 'Stacksteads and Laneside Branch'. This road runs parallel to the 1789 road but keeps to the valley bottom via Waterfoot and Laneside, and is now the main route through Rossendale.

During the turnpike era the importance of road stucture and surface condition became more widely understood. John Metcalf, who built sections of the Burnley to Skipton and the Bury to Whalley roads, as well as several other roads in Lancashire and Yorkshire, recognised the necessity for firm foundations, especially on boggy ground. John Macadam emphasised the importance of a well-drained firm surface; he built part of the 1815 Rossendale road mentioned above.

The turnpike era has left little behind in the way of visible remains. The turnpikes form the basis of the modern road network and continuous widening, straightening, and resurfacing has gradually transformed their character. The milestones erected by the trusts sometimes still remain by the roadside, especially in the Halifax and Keighley areas.

Some tollhouses or 'bars' can still be found, now often occupied as dwellings or public houses (Fig 51). The system of tolls was complex, frequently depending upon the weight of the vehicle or its wheel size. There were many classes of exemptions from toll; coal was often carried at lower tolls to promote its freer movement since many turnpike trustees were also coal owners. The tollhouses themselves normally jut out into the road to allow the gatekeeper a watchful eye on passing traffic. Steanor Bottom Bar on the Rochdale to Todmorden road is a good example. It is a six-sided two-storey structure which formerly bore a board displaying the list of charges. The Old Toll Bar Inn at the foot of Fecitt Brow in Blackburn is a former tollhouse dating from about

51    Toll house at Barrowford, Pendle. It formerly carried boards displaying the list of charges.

1830. Another Toll Bar Inn in Blackburn stood at the junction of the Whalley Old and New Roads, but this was demolished some years ago.

The turnpike era ended with the coming of the railways in the 1840s. From that time there was little road development until the growth in motor traffic after 1920 stimulated a further generation of road building which is still continuing.

## The old roads of Blackstone Edge

A Rochdale scholar, James Maxim, was particularly fascinated by the series of old roads which cross the main Pennine watershed from Rochdale to Halifax by way of the high ridge of Blackstone Edge. His interest in this subject extended throughout his life, and he spent much of his spare time out of doors searching for evidence of the origin of these roads. He never published a full account of his work, but a small book summarising his findings was produced after his death.

Maxim found that no fewer than four routes had been used to cross this part of the Pennines (Fig 52). The most recent is the present A58 motor road, originally a turnpike road constructed under the Fourth Blackstone Edge Turnpike Trust Act of 1795. Maxim called this the 'New Road' since on the Lancashire side of the boundary it superseded an 'Old Road' constructed under the Third Turnpike Trust Act of 1765. Part of the Old Road is now disused and is traceable only as a footpath.

52   Old roads on Blackstone Edge (after Maxim). This ridge forming the main divide of the central Pennines has been crossed by four different roads at various times in history.

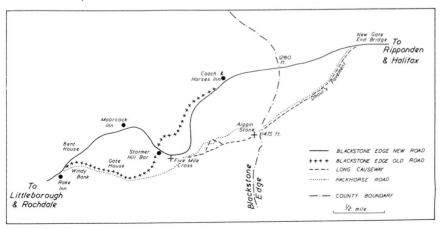

It was however the pre-turnpike roads which especially interested Maxim. He traced the course of a packhorse road from the outskirts of Littleborough, round Stormer Hill, and up on to the Edge where it crosses over into Yorkshire at 1,475 ft. The lower part of the Packhorse Road was followed by the Old Road, but elsewhere it took the form of a narrow paved track no more than 3 ft wide winding up the steep face of the Edge, a climb of 600 ft in less than a mile. Stone cross bases along the route testify to its antiquity. In 1291 Richard de Radeclive and Hugh de Elaund were granted permission to levy custom on goods carried over *Blakesteynegge* for repairing the causeway, and it is almost certainly this road to which the grant relates. Celia Fiennes, travelling this road in the seventeenth century, found it 'steep in the ascent and descent on either end', while another traveller from Halifax in 1639 thought he 'had been in the land of break-neck, it was so steep and tedious and past repair'. Defoe, crossing Blackstone Edge in August about 1720 found the way 'frightful, narrow and precipitous'. With the advent of the coaching era the road quickly became inadequate and was thus superseded by the Old Road which crosses the Edge some 200 ft lower and thus has considerably easier gradients.

There is however a fourth road on Blackstone Edge, and it was to this that Maxim gave most attention. This road begins alongside the Packhorse Road close to the eastern track to Blackstone Edge Fold. It ascends to the same point on the Edge as the Packhorse Road but by a straighter route. On the Yorkshire side it follows the Packhorse Road as far as the junction with the New Road. This road, termed by Maxim the 'Long Causeway', is up to 16 ft wide and consists mostly of sandstone setts, slightly cambered, resting upon sand and rubble, and with a central line of troughed stones. On the Yorkshire side it terminates as the 'Dhoul's Pavement', a natural rock surface some 20 ft wide.

This road is marked on the Ordnance Survey maps as a Roman road, but Maxim believed that a Roman origin was unlikely. He could find little evidence of Roman construction in the Long Causeway or other sections of a possible Roman road elsewhere around Rochdale. He also discovered a 'loop' from the road a quarter of a mile east of its origin and clearly built at the same time as the main Causeway. This loop passes on top of the Packhorse Road, indicating that the latter must have been built first. Maxim concluded that the Causeway was probably built under the First Turnpike Trust Act of 1735. The 'loop' was perhaps a passing place, very necessary on the steep slope of the Edge. After the construction of the Old Road soon after 1766 the Causeway probably fell into disuse.

# The canal builders

Canals grew out of the failure of the eighteenth century road system to move the growing volume of traffic which the surge of the Industrial Revolution created. The ancestors of canals were the river navigations. In the early eighteenth century the Calder was made navigable to Wakefield and by 1740 merchants in the Halifax area were demanding its upstream extension in order to cheapen the cost of wool and grain to the region from Lincolnshire and East Anglia. This extension, completed as the Calder and Hebble Navigation in 1770, was the prelude to a phase of canal construction in the Pennines. Economic necessity overrode the difficult physical conditions, and between 1773 and 1816 the Pennines were spanned by three canals linking together the growing industrial areas.

The most successful of the three was the Rochdale Canal, built by William Jessop and completed in 1804 from Manchester to Sowerby Bridge where it joined the Calder & Hebble. On the Lancashire side it linked with the Bridgewater Canal which supplied it with coal, stone, salt, and timber to be carried to the industrial valleys around Rochdale and Todmorden; in the opposite direction came grain from Lincolnshire and coal from Yorkshire.

South of the Rochdale the Huddersfield Canal linked the two counties by a more direct but less used route. This was a narrow boat canal with a smaller capacity than the Rochdale. It carried mainly merchandise, with coal as the main bulk item. North of the Rochdale the Pennines were bridged by the circuitous Leed & Liverpool Canal. The construction of the Leeds & Liverpool, the first of the three canals to be started and the last to be completed, was continually plagued by shortages of capital, and by the time it was finished in 1816 the canal building age was already past its zenith. It carried little through traffic, most movements being confined to either side of the summit level. Its principal cargo in the Pennine area was limestone, carried from quarries in the Craven area to limekilns between Skipton and Bradford and in the Burnley district.

The canal builders each had different ideas about the most suitable width for a canal. 'Narrow boat' canals with locks taking boats up to 7 ft wide, were cheaper to build per mile than broad canals and were more economical of water, but their limited capacity meant that they were soon unable to cope with the volume of traffic generated by the Industrial Revolution. 'Broad' canals could take boats 14 ft wide and could therefore be used by river barges, and the Rochdale and Leeds & Liverpool were of this type. Huddersfield became a transhipment point where traffic from the narrow Huddersfield Canal was transferred to the broader barges of the three-mile Sir John Ramsden's Canal which joined the Calder & Hebble Navigation. Sowerby Bridge, the terminus of both the Rochdale Canal and the Calder & Hebble Navigation, grew as another transhipment point because barges from the Rochdale were unable to negotiate the shorter locks of the navigation (Fig 53).

Although the technology of canals may now appear to be primitive, nevertheless the accomplishments of the canal builders were considerable when judged by the engineering knowledge of two centuries ago. The main tools of the navigator or 'navvie' were the shovel and wheelbarrow; the previous experience of the contractor was commonly limited to building ships, repairing water mills, or draining mines. It is hardly surprising that when the canals were completed they were regarded as new wonders of the world.

Gradient provided the engineer with his most perplexing problem. The many gradients of the Pennine canal routes had to be surmounted by going round, building locks, or tunnelling. Each solution presented a greater degree of technical complexity and therefore cost, but an increasingly direct and speedier route. To avoid gradients by following the contours was often impossible, and all trans-Pennine canals were heavily locked, the Rochdale having ninety-two locks in its thirty-three

53 Sowerby Bridge was a transhipment point at the meeting of the Rochdale Canal and Calder & Hebble Navigation. Locks on the Calder & Hebble Navigation were shorter than those on the Rochdale Canal and could take only smaller vessels.

miles. Sometimes locking is concentrated at points of especially steep gradient. At Wheelton near Blackburn the Leeds & Liverpool drops 60 ft by a flight of seven locks; at Bingley the same canal ascends Airedale by the 'Five-Rise' staircase, again of 60 ft.

Tunnelling was difficult and costly. The Rochdale managed to avoid tunnels altogether, but the Leeds & Liverpool has tunnels at Burnley and Foulridge. The most impressive tunnel however is the Standedge tunnel on the Huddersfield Canal. It crosses the 1,300 ft watershed at a summit height of 648 ft, the highest canal summit in Britain. Its length of 3 miles 176 yds makes it Britain's longest canal tunnel, and it took fifteen years to build. The tunnel is only 9 ft wide with four passing places. As was common practice, no towpath was provided and the boat was 'legged' through by the boatman lying on his back and moving the boat by pushing his feet against the tunnel roof.

Tunnel construction utilised techniques learned in mining. Along the route, shafts about 8 ft in diameter were sunk at intervals below the intended tunnel level. From these a drainage channel or culvert was constructed emptying into a convenient stream to drain off the ground water and lower the water table. After drainage the main bore was constructed, starting at both ends and also working from the shafts which provided access, waste spoil removal points, and ventilation. The tunnel was then lined with timber and stone. Most of the work was done by pick-axe and spade in candlelight, and men often had to labour in several feet of water.

Water supply was another problem which troubled the canal builders, particularly where the canals crossed major watersheds. Reservoirs were built to supply the canals, but in dry summers summit stretches frequently ran empty and through navigation ceased. The Leeds & Liverpool, which crossed the permeable limestone country of Craven, was especially vulnerable and during the dry years of the 1880s functioned as two separate stretches on either side of the summit. The original three reservoirs of the Rochdale Canal grew eventually to eight. The largest, the 130-acre Hollingworth Lake, became a popular pleasure spot in Victorian times.

A walk along the Leeds & Liverpool towpath in the Burnley area reveals many of the features of the Pennine canalside scene. The canal enters Burnley from the west by the 559 yd Gannow Tunnel, built by Robert Whitworth and Samuel Fletcher and opened in 1801 after five years of construction. Stone masons have carved strange hieroglyphics at both ends of the tunnel and on nearby Gannow Bridge (Fig 54). A mile eastwards is the Burnley wharf at Manchester Road. This was one of the main wharves on the Leeds & Liverpool and provided Burnley's main warehousing in the early nineteenth century. Flour, sugar, cotton, lime,

54   The Gannow Tunnel on the Leeds & Liverpool Canal, Burnley. Stonemasons' marks decorate the tunnel entrance.

and malt were important commodities stored here. The warehouse has a wooden canopy over the wharf and stables in the yard at the rear. It was also a toll collection point on the canal and the toll house is still preserved. Around the wharf can be seen minor canalside features; an incline into the canal for pulling out horses, rope marks on the stonework, and a guidewheel around which towropes were wound. East of the wharfeage the canal then crosses the river Calder by the 1,256 yd Burnley Embankment, which dominates the centre of Burnley and provides a fine view of this Lancashire industrial townscape. Some 350,000 cu yd of earth, most of which came from the Gannow tunnel, went into the construction of the embankment.

## Pennine railways

The supremacy of the canal was short-lived. Fourteen years after the last lock on the Leeds & Liverpool Canal had been opened for traffic, a new mode of transport arrived in Lancashire to announce the canal's obsolescence. The battle between railway and canal was short and decisive. The railway won because it could do everything the canal could do and a great deal more, as well as doing it more quickly. By 1850 the railway had established its tentacles in every nook of the Pennines, and for the next seventy years it was to provide the arteries of the region.

The traffic patterns of the Pennine railway age reflected the economic geography of the period. The textile industry generated the movement of a vast number of mill workers each day, as well as of raw cotton and finished fabrics. The principal freight traffic was coal, hauled to the mill towns and to Liverpool and Hull for export. Physical conditions made the carriage of all this traffic by no means easy, for the system included numerous steep gradients and tight curves.

Since its heyday the Pennine railway network has suffered its share of contraction. Because of the severe decline of the industries on which it depended, the contraction has been proportionately greater than in some other parts of the country. The present network is only a skeleton of the original, linking the principal industrial towns with Manchester and Leeds. The Aire gap route is now closed to trains from east Lancashire while the Burnley-Todmorden trans-Pennine link sees only occasional passenger trains. Indeed, the railway map of the 1970s is strikingly similar to that of 1850 (Fig 55).

To yesterday's rail traveller, the most noteworthy features of the Pennine railway scene were the many bridges, viaducts, and tunnels built to cope with the often severe relief. The highest point on the system was Trough Gate at 965 ft on the Rochdale to Bacup line, and at several other places heights exceeding 700 ft were reached. Some 110 miles of track were at gradients exceeding 1 in 100, the steepest being the 1 in 27 Werneth incline from Middleton Junction to Oldham, which for a short time after its completion required cable haulage. The East Lancashire Railway line from Bury to Accrington climbed at 1 in 78 for most of the way from Ramsbottom to the summit of the line at Baxenden before dropping via a 1 in 40 incline the two miles into Accrington. The hilly situation of Halifax necessitated approaches by gradients in some cases exceeding 1 in 60.

There are some forty tunnels in the area shown on the map. Most are short stretches of only one or two hundred yards. Longer tunnels are invariably associated with the crossing of major watersheds. This is the case with the Sough tunnel, which crosses the divide between the Ribble and Mersey, the Summit tunnel between the Irwell and Yorkshire Calder, and the three-mile-long Standedge tunnel which runs parallel to the canal tunnel beneath the main Pennine axis. The deeply incised nature of Pennine valleys means that bridges and viaducts are very much

139

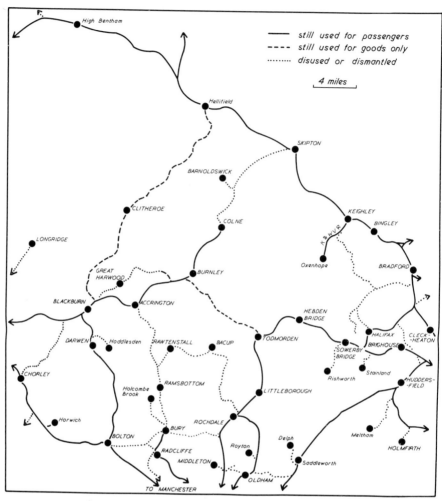

55  Pennine railway network, past and present. Few villages were more than four miles from a railway station.

in evidence; there are four major viaducts and thirty bridges as well as six tunnels on the thirteen mile Huddersfield to Penistone route. Throughout the Pennines viaducts sweep across town centres, adding discordant but distinctive lines to the townscapes, as at Accrington and Burnley.

Railway journeys are often a valuable way of discovering the main features of a region's character and scenery. A small-scale Pennine panorama can be observed by a journey from Bolton to Blackburn, one of the few remaining minor routes. The thirteen-mile line, completed in

1848 with seven intermediate stations, used to carry Midland Railway services between Manchester and Scotland via Hellifield as well as the local Lancashire & Yorkshire Railway services. It is now mostly single-tracked with only three intermediate stations.

The railway leaves Bolton by the Croal and Tonge viaducts which give a characteristic view of a Lancashire cotton town landscape, including the terminal basin of the Manchester, Bolton, & Bury Canal. The line soon begins to climb steeply at 1 in 74, a gradient maintained for five miles. Bromley Cross, the first stop, has a pleasant rural atmosphere and is one of the few manned minor stations remaining in east Lancashire. Beyond Bromley Cross the gradient becomes more noticeable and the Pennine scenery dominant. There are fine views to the right across Wayoh Reservoir towards the moors beyond Edgworth. This section of the line is also noteworthy for its attractive turreted overbridges near Turton Tower (Fig 56). The railway next serves the wayside halt at Entwistle beyond which the trackbed widens, for there were once sidings here serving a quarry half a mile away on the hillside feeding the railway by a tramroad.

Beyond this old siding the line becomes encased by a deep cutting as

56 Railway bridge at Turton Tower. The owner of the house insisted on the building of this ornate bridge to provide access to grounds beyond the railway. One turret contains a stone staircase and seat.

the summit is reached at 800 ft. The line then plunges down at 1 in 75 into the 2,000 yd Sough Tunnel, the greatest engineering work on the line, emerging into another grim cutting at the Darwen end. As the train takes the curve down the valley, there is a striking view across the mill town of Darwen, with its sandstone-fronted streets clinging to the hillsides, to the open moor beyond crowned at 1,225 ft by the now restored Jubilee Tower of 1898. Beyond Darwen the gradient slackens and the view is increasingly urban and industrial; as Blackburn is approached mills and defunct mill chimneys compete for height with the high-rise blocks of flats of later generations. The journey now takes 25 minutes compared with 54 in 1858; at that date the four miles from the Oaks to the summit at the Sough Tunnell alone took nearly 25 minutes. Heavy trains using the line invariably needed banking assistance.

Steam traction today survives in the central Pennines on the privately owned Worth Valley Railway which in summer and at weekends runs a regular service between Keighley, Haworth, and Oxenhope.

**Selected further reading**:

W. Albert, *The Turnpike Road System in England, 1663-1840*, Cambridge, 1972

W. B. Crump, 'Ancient Highways of the Parish of Halifax', *Transactions of the Halifax Antiquarian Society*, 1924-9

W. B. Crump, 'Saltways from the Cheshire Wiches', *Transactions of the Lancashire & Cheshire Antiquarian Society*, vol 54, 1939

C. Hadfield, *The Canals of Yorkshire and North-East England*, David & Charles, 1972

C. Hadfield & G. Biddle, *The Canals of North-West England*, David & Charles, 1970

J. Marshall, *The Lancashire & Yorkshire Railway*, David & Charles, 1969

J. Maxim, *A Lancashire Lion*, Leeds, 1965

A. Raistrick, *Green Roads in the Mid-Pennines*, Moorland, 1978

# 11 New Pressures: Conserving the Heritage

By the first decade of the twentieth century the pulse of economic expansion had slowed considerably. Population growth, which in the previous century had quadrupled or quintupled the size of many settlements, was now proceeding at a much reduced rate, and for many towns the zenith of population size was passed by 1920. Few new mills were built after 1910, and by the 1920s the textile industry was in clear recession. Competition from the Far East reduced the industry's export effectiveness, and to this was added the more general economic stagnation of the inter-war years. The cotton textile regions felt the recession hardest. The industry never recovered, and the decline has continued through to the present day. Coal mining, a second staple industry, was already in decline by the later nineteenth century and has now almost completely left the region. Industrial recession has been accompanied by a decline in rural economic activity, the Pennines sharing in the more general retreat during the last century of the country's agriculture from the moorland margins.

Economic decline has brought changes in social and economic structure. Old industrial districts, particularly those heavily dependent on the textile trade, have lost population steadily throughout the century and tend to have a relatively ageing population. Todmorden, in the centre of the region, lost 37 per cent of its population between 1921 and 1971. Those industrial areas which have escaped steady population decline have done so only by considerably broadening their industrial base. The urban landscape readily betrays evidence of economic stagnation; demolished or derelict mills, abandoned quarries, boarded up shops, rarely used public buildings, and chapels converted to warehouses are common sights and all point to declining communities. Population loss has also characterised the remoter upland areas. Here the forestry and water supply industries are now more important employers than farming.

The more accessible rural areas on the fringes of the larger towns show different trends, for here a renewal of population has become evident in post-war years. This has largely resulted from migration into these districts by car-borne commuters with jobs in the neighbouring towns, and many old villages now have new housing developments alongside older traditional properties. Urban fringes have also expanded into the surrounding countryside as inner urban redevelopment schemes have created a need for modern low density housing on the outskirts. In Halifax modern housing development at Illingworth and Mixenden has eaten into the edge of the moors above Luddenden, while villages such as Egerton and Bromley Cross have become commuter suburbs of Bolton.

With the coming of the twentieth century man has placed new demands upon the central Pennines. The continued growth of the Lancashire and Yorkshire conurbations has put ever increasing pressure on the region's water resources, so that today some seventy reservoirs are needed to supply this demand and a sixth of the area of the region is devoted to water catchment. The growing utilisation of these water resources has had considerable implications for rural settlement and agriculture. The flooding of valleys consumes the better quality land and reduces the amount of pasture for cattle and winter feed for sheep. Farmsteads sometimes have to be abandoned. Wider depopulation occurs in the gathering grounds around the reservoir where livestock grazing has to be restricted or prohibited. In some cases entire valley communities have disappeared to make way for reservoirs and their catchment areas (Fig 57). This occurred in the upper Hodder valley north of Slaidburn. Between 1923 and 1932 the construction of the Stocks Reservoir at the head of this valley involved the building of a

57 Haslingden Grane was a flourishing weaving community in the nineteenth century. Reservoir building has been responsible for the district's almost total depopulation.

144

440yd dam behind which were submerged 244 acres of pasture. The hamlet of Stocks-in-Bowland and four nearby farms disappeared beneath the reservoir, while the small chapel of Dalehead was dismantled and rebuilt half a mile away. In the surrounding catchment area twenty-six outlying farms and cottages were abandoned. The gathering grounds now contain the Forestry Commission's largest plantation in the mid-Pennines, some 3,700 acres of conifers.

The chief new pressure on the Pennine uplands however has come from the growth of population in surrounding urban areas and its improved means of access to the region. The growth of private car ownership and road improvement schemes have brought a much greater population within shorter travelling times of the upland landscape. Popular beauty spots along the main Pennine axis such as Hardcastle Crags have up to 6 million people living within an hour's journey. The results are most readily seen on Sunday afternoons in summer; the narrow pass of the Trough of Bowland, deserted in the winter months, experiences a steady stream of cars, and vacant parking spaces between Dunsop Bridge and Abbeystead are hard to find. The growth of private motoring has brought an increased awareness of the region's leisure potential not merely to its local population but on a wider scale; tourism, at present mostly restricted to weekend visitors and to better known localities such as Haworth, is nevertheless a growth industry, and improvement of amenities for day and weekend trippers will enhance the attractiveness of the area to longer stay tourists.

Certainly there is much to see. A landscape survey by the former West Riding County Council classified the higher parts of the main central Pennine axis and the Forest of Bowland as areas of 'great landscape quality', and much of the western Pennine moorland between Blackburn and Bolton not included in the survey would qualify for the same category. This is the real Pennine wilderness, a vestige of the region's once far more extensive wildscape. Scenery described by the survey as 'attractive' occupies the lower uplands, the Ribble valley, and the Craven district. Built-up areas are continuous only between Halifax and Bradford and on the fringe of the Manchester conurbation; elsewhere urban development is discontinuous and many urban dwellers live within a few minutes' drive of fine open country.

To the quality of the physical landscape man has added his own contribution. The man-made landscape is the product of two millennia of human occupation of the region; it contains not everything that man has added to the landscape in that time, but only those features which he has both added and found useful to retain — or at least not to dispense with. The Victorian legacy, part of the comparatively recent past, is now of greater interest to visitor and historian alike, particularly as an

**58** The central Pennines: landscape heritage. Many of the sites shown have been the subject of earlier chapters of this book. Conservation of the past increasingly has to be reconciled with growing recreational pressures.

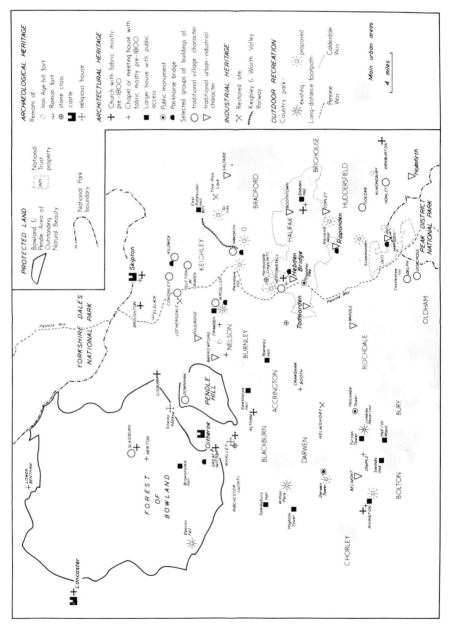

increasing proportion of it is disappearing under the bulldozer. The pre-factory era is well represented by the many weavers' cottages and farmhouses with their distinctively vernacular styles. Less remains from the medieval period because only certain parts of the region were closely settled at this time, but there is nevertheless a fair sprinkling of old churches and largely unaltered medieval villages.

Some districts are particularly well endowed with remains of the past. The northern fringes of Bolton and the moors beyond have examples of villages dating from the early factory era. Between Huddersfield and Oldham villages such as Honley, Dobcross, and Delph, with their all-stone roofscapes surmounting rows of weavers' windows are fully representative of Pennine settlements of the hand-loom weaving era. Possibly the most interesting single settlement is Heptonstall, which besides its many stone cottages and twisting streets can count its ruined medieval church, cloth hall, and octagonal chapel as major architectural attractions. It has strong associations with the Civil War and with early Methodism and gains appeal from its position high on an eminence overlooking the Calder valley. Haworth, a few miles further north, has a scarcely less interesting fabric but is mostly known for its Brontë connections. The Keighley and Worth Valley Railway, an attractive leisure feature in itself, reinforces the status of Haworth as the region's most important single tourist location. Eastwards into Craven and Bowland and down the Ribble valley the emphasis is different; these areas escaped most of the Industrial Revolution and the medieval heritage is most evident. Here there are examples of pre-Reformation churches and medieval villages such as Downham and Waddington, the layout and character of which have changed little in recent centuries.

The growth of interest in the region and its cultural heritage has gone side by side with a greater concern by authorities towards planning for conservation and leisure. In 1964 300 square miles of the Forest of Bowland, including Pendle Hill and its environs, were designated an Area of Outstanding Natural Beauty, a status which helps to restrict undesirable development. In 1973 local authorities examined the idea of creating a South Pennine Park recreational area southwards from Skipton through Craven and the Calder and Colne valley areas to the boundary of the Peak District National Park. This scheme aimed to conserve sites of historical and landscape interest and to develop varied types of leisure amenity to meet the increasing recreational demands on the region. Although the Park concept itself is not now to be imple-mented, provision of several of the amenities associated with it has gone ahead. Further westwards the most recent proposal is for the establish-ment of a West Pennine Moors recreational zone covering the uplands bounded by Blackburn, Accrington, Bolton, and Chorley, and with similar objectives to the South Pennine plan. This scheme foresees the channelling of outdoor leisure pursuits into three 'Recreational Managment Zones' in the Anglezarke, Darwen Moor, and Jumbles Reservoir areas.

Some of the more tangible results of recreational planning have now appeared. Much of the central Pennines is crossed by the Pennine Way long-distance footpath, which forms a thread linking many of the area's most important landscape features. It crosses fine National Trust moors above Marsden and descends from Stoodley Pike into the Calder valley to pass close to the Heptonstall-Hardcastle Crags area and to Hebden Bridge, now being developed as the focal tourist information point of the mid-Pennines. It traverses Brontë country close to Haworth before descending into the picturesque Craven area round Lothersdale on its way to the Yorkshire Dales. Another recently created footpath is the Calderdale Way, a circular route which joins many places of landscape interest in the Calder valley region around Hebden Bridge and Halifax.

Several picnic sites and country parks have been laid out. The former

59  Canalside scene at Skipton. Pleasure cruising is a popular pastime on the Leeds and Liverpool Canal.

normally provide basic amenities such as parking space, a walking area, and toilets, but the country parks are more extensive and have a wider range of leisure facilities. Beacon Fell, 8 miles north of Preston on the southern edge of the Forest of Bowland, was Lancashire's first country park, opened in 1970. It provides 269 acres of coniferous woods and moorlands with forest walks, picnic points, and wide views from its 873 ft high summit. Access roads have been provided and there is parking space for 400 cars. The aim of the park is 'the creation and maintenance of a balanced composition of woodland, field, and open fell conducive to … outdoor leisure pursuits of a quiet and informal nature … whilst at the same time giving the public access to prominent viewpoints not usually accessible by motor car'. Another country park is at Wycoller, within a few minutes' drive of the Burnley-Colne urban area. Here the emphasis is on the man-made heritage as well as the natural landscape, for the focus of this 352-acre recreation area is the ruins of the seventeenth-century weaving hamlet. A ring of country parks is being created in the Haworth area, both to relieve the pressure on this village and to serve the leisure needs of Bradford and Keighley.

The Scammonden valley exemplifies the new pressures to which man is subjecting the central Pennines in the second half of the twentieth century. Until the 1960s this was a quiet farming community. The M62 now crosses the valley by means of a 2,000 ft-long viaduct which carries traffic 240 ft above the valley floor. Behind the dam are impounded up to 1,730 million gallons of water in a 104-acre reservoir. The site has attracted growing interest as a leisure amenity. Many visitors come to admire the scale of the project and to watch the sailing or motoring club, while for others the attraction lies in the combination of water, views and open moorland. Seventy acres of deciduous and coniferous woodland have been planted on the reservoir slopes in small irregular plots to add variety to the scene. When these are mature the locality will be able to absorb more visitors less obtrusively. Yet nowhere is the tranquility alongside Scammonden Water entirely free from the steady drone of vehicles on the viaduct. The many uses of Scammonden — water, transport, forestry, and recreation — are a constant reminder of the need to make fuller use of the environment without damaging it, and of man's never ceasing pressures on the central Pennine landscape.

**Selected further reading**:

*The Pennine Uplands: Socio-economic Interactions and Opportunities in the Yorkshire Pennines*, Yorkshire and Humberside Economic Planning Board, 1975

*Recreation in the South Pennines: an Interim Report*, West Riding County Council, 1973

*West Pennine Moors Local Plan – Approach to a Plan*, Lancashire County Council, 1978

# Index